DAN S...

A SPECTATOR'S GUIDE TO BASKETBALL

For:
Would-be fans
Friends and spouses of basketball fanatics
Parents of basketball players
In short, anyone who doesn't know a forward from a guard, and would like to learn

Other Avon Books by
Dan Sperling

A SPECTATOR'S GUIDE TO BASEBALL
A SPECTATOR'S GUIDE TO FOOTBALL

Avon Books are available at special quantity discounts for bulk purchases for sales promotions, premiums, fund raising or educational use. Special books, or book excerpts, can also be created to fit specific needs.

For details write or telephone the office of the Director of Special Markets, Avon Books, Dept. FP, 1790 Broadway, New York, New York 10019, 212-399-1357.

A SPECTATOR'S GUIDE TO BASKETBALL

THE ACTION, RULES, AND BEAUTY OF THE GAME

DAN SPERLING

AVON
PUBLISHERS OF BARD, CAMELOT, DISCUS AND FLARE BOOKS

A SPECTATOR'S GUIDE TO BASKETBALL: *The Action, Rules, and Beauty of the Game* is an original publication of Avon Books. This work has never before appeared in book form.

Grateful acknowledgment is made for use of the following art and photographs:

#2, Courtesy of Wilson Sporting Goods Co.; #3, 4, Allen Sperling; #5, Steve Carter, Courtesy of the Boston Celtics; #6, Marv Parent, Courtesy of the Detroit Pistons; #7, Courtesy of the Phoenix Suns; #8, Rodney E. Raschke, Courtesy of the Los Angeles Lakers; #9, 16, Joey Beninato, Courtesy of the Phoenix Suns; #10, Charles Cyr, Courtesy of the San Antonio Spurs; #11, Courtesy of the Denver Nuggets; #12, Ray Foley, Courtesy of the Boston Celtics; #13, 15, Gary Fine, Courtesy of the Washington Bullets; #14, Courtesy of the Los Angeles Lakers; #17, Bill Smith, Courtesy of the Chicago Bulls

AVON BOOKS
A division of
The Hearst Corporation
1790 Broadway
New York, New York 10019

Copyright © 1983 by Dan Sperling
Published by arrangement with the author
Library of Congress Catalog Card Number: 83-91106
ISBN: 0-380-85191-1

All rights reserved, which includes the right to reproduce this book or portions thereof in any form whatsoever except as provided by the U. S. Copyright Law. For information address Audrey Wolf, 1000 Potomac Street NW, Suite 105, Washington, D.C. 20007

First Avon Printing, November, 1983

AVON TRADEMARK REG. U. S. PAT. OFF. AND IN OTHER COUNTRIES, MARCA REGISTRADA, HECHO EN U. S. A.

Printed in the U. S. A.

WFH 10 9 8 7 6 5 4 3 2 1

To A. R. A., with gratitude

For their help:

Thanks to the National Basketball Association and the University of Maryland basketball program—and to the many NBA teams that provided photographs. Special thanks to my father, Allen Sperling.

TABLE OF CONTENTS

INTRODUCTION		11
NOTE TO THE READER		13
CHAPTER 1:	What Basketball is All About	15
CHAPTER 2:	Offense	33
CHAPTER 3:	Defense	44
CHAPTER 4:	The Beauty of the Game: Some Things to Look For	51
CHAPTER 5:	The NBA	56
CHAPTER 6:	College Basketball	59
CHAPTER 7:	International Rules	64
CHAPTER 8:	Box Scores, Standings, and Statistics	66
CHAPTER 9:	History	72
GLOSSARY		77
INDEX		91

INTRODUCTION

This book is for anyone who knows little or nothing about basketball, and who would like to understand the game without wading through page after page of confusing nonessentials and unexplained jargon. It contains everything the reader needs to know to comprehend and enjoy basketball—live or broadcast—as a spectator. Its language is concise and matter-of-fact, presenting the fundamentals of the game clearly and simply, in as few words as possible. Its only promise is that reading it will make the world's most widely played sport a thousand times simpler—and ten thousand times more enjoyable.

NOTE TO THE READER

Basketball is basically one game, regardless of where it's played. Its rules differ very little from league to league and from level to level. For simplicity's sake, all assertions in this book refer to professional basketball as played in the National Basketball Association (NBA), unless otherwise indicated. Chapters 6 and 7 highlight the minor differences between NBA basketball and the game as played collegiately and outside the United States.

CHAPTER 1
What Basketball Is All About

THE GAME IN GENERAL

A basketball game is a timed contest between two teams, each consisting of five players plus substitutes. It is played in an indoor arena on a rectangular hardwood *court*, or playing area, that is ninety-four feet long and fifty feet wide (see illustration 1). All territory outside this rectangle is considered *out of bounds*, or outside the playing area; while all territory within the rectangle is considered *in bounds*, or within the playing area. The court's two longest boundaries are called *sidelines*, and its two shorter boundaries are called *end lines*, or *baselines*. These boundary lines are themselves considered out of bounds. Other court markings will be explained shortly.

The game is played with a round, inflated, bounceable ball (or *basketball*) that is twenty-nine and one-half inches to thirty inches in circumference, from twenty to twenty-two ounces in weight, and covered with pebble-grained leather (see illustration 2). The central idea in basketball is to score *points* by throwing the ball through a *basket* or (*hoop*)—one of two horizontal metal rings eighteen inches in diameter, suspended ten feet above the floor at the ends of the court (see illustrations 1 and 3). The team with the most points at the end of the game wins. A team can score points only by throwing the ball through its own assigned basket, and the ball must pass downward through the hoop. An attempt to throw the ball through a basket is called a *shot*, and a player who has attempted a shot is said to have *shot the ball* (or simply to have *shot*).

Each basket is attached to an upright, rectangular slab of clear glass called the *backboard*, which measures four feet high and six feet across and is supported by a curved base standing several feet out of bounds (see illustration 4). Each backboard is perpendicular to the floor, parallel to the baseline, and equidistant from the sidelines. Its plane intersects the court floor four feet inside the end line. The backboards are transparent for the benefit of spectators seated behind them, and are intended to support the baskets, to deflect shots into the hoops, and to deflect errant shots back onto the court.

An important rule in basketball stipulates that the ball cannot be carried or intentionally kicked from one position on the court to another, but must be either *passed* (that is, thrown to another player) or continuously bounced against the court surface with either hand by a player as he moves (see illustration 5). Bouncing the ball against the court is called *dribbling*. A *pass* (i.e., a thrown ball) can bounce any number of times, or not at all, before being legally caught.

Whenever a team has possession of the ball, that team is said to be *on offense*, and the opposing team is said to be *on defense*. (The ball changes team possession constantly during the course of a game, often several times a minute.) The defensive players, or *defenders*, try to prevent the offensive players from scoring by *blocking* (i.e., deflecting or obstructing) their shots (see illustration 6). Defenders also try to gain possession of the ball by *stealing* it (that is, by taking it away from an opponent who is holding or dribbling it, or by intercepting a pass). A defender's overall task is made somewhat difficult by the fact that no player is allowed to hold, strike, push, or trip an opponent, or to impede his progress by extending the arms.

The length of a basketball game is normally forty-eight minutes of official playing time, as determined by a large digital stop-clock called the *game clock* (or simply the *clock*), which is located where players and spectators can see it easily. The game clock does not run continuously, but stops and starts according to rules that will be explained shortly. A game usually lasts about two hours, and its forty-eight minutes of official playing time are divided into four twelve-minute *periods*, which are also known as *quarters*. A *buzzer* or *horn* sounds to indicate the end of each period. The first and second periods constitute the game's *first half*, and the third and fourth periods constitute the *second half*. A fifteen-minute intermission known as *halftime*—during which there is normally some sort of on-court entertainment for the spectators—follows the second period. If the score is tied after forty-eight minutes of play, the game continues for an additional five-minute period, called *overtime*. If the score is tied at the end of this overtime period, a second five-minute overtime period is played, and so on until there is a winner. There are no ties in basketball.

The team on whose court the game is played is called the *home team*, and is said to be playing *at home*. The other team is known as the *visiting team* (or *visitors*), and a said to be playing *away*, or *on the road*. The visiting team gets its choice of baskets to shoot at for the first half of the game. The teams switch baskets at the end of the first half, but do not switch again in the event of overtime.

Each basketball game is presided over by two *officials*, or *referees* (see illustration 7), who enforce, interpret, and apply the rules. The officials carry loud whistles, which they blow to stop *play (game action)* when necessary. Any ruling made by an official is known as a *call*. An official who makes a call involving an infraction is said to have *called* that particular infraction *on* the guilty player or team, who is said to have been *called for* the infraction.

HANDLING THE BALL

As was previously stated, a *ball handler* (i.e., a player in possession of the ball during game action) is not permitted to move from one spot on the court to another without dribbling. A violation of this rule—that is, the illegal act of carrying the ball instead of dribbling it— is called *traveling* (or *walking*, or *carrying*, or *steps*). Traveling awards the ball to the other team, as does any other rule infraction on the part of an offensive player.

A player dribbling the ball is not permitted to touch it more than once per bounce, or to touch it with both hands simultaneously (although he may alternate hands on different bounces). A violation of either of these rules is called a *double-dribble*. A player who stops dribbling (i.e., who catches the ball after bouncing it) must either pass or shoot; he can't begin dribbling again. A violation of this rule is also called a double-dribble.

A ball handler who is not dribbling is permitted to step with the same foot in any direction any number of times—provided his other foot, called his *pivot foot*, does not move from its spot on the floor (although it may pivot, or rotate on its vertical axis). However, a moving dribbler is allowed to complete the step in progress as his dribble is terminated, and take one additional step before coming to a stop or getting rid of the ball. A ball handler who leaves his feet must either pass or shoot before landing, and a player cannot touch his own pass or shot until the ball has touched the basket or backboard, or another player.

FIELD GOALS

A successful shot taken during game action is called a *field goal* (or *basket*), and its shooter is said to have *made* the shot (or to have made a basket or field goal, or simply to have *scored*).

For a shot to be ruled successful, the ball must pass

downward through the basket, and can be either thrown or tapped with the hand. A field goal that is tapped into the basket is called a *tap-in*, or *tap* (or *tip-in*, or *tip*), and one that's thrown or shoved downward through the hoop from directly above it (by a very tall or very high-leaping player) is called a *dunk*, *slam-dunk*, *slam-jam*, or *stuff*.

A field goal normally awards two points to the shooter's team. However, a field goal is worth three points instead of two if the shot is taken from behind the *three-point line*, which consists of an on-court arc curving 23.75 feet from a point directly under the center of the basket, and tapering to straight lines that run parallel with the sidelines at a distance of three feet all the way to the baseline (see illustration 1). If a player inadvertently puts the ball through the opposing team's basket, it counts as a field goal for the opposing team.

If a period ends while a successful shot is in flight, the shot counts as a field goal—since the ball left the shooter's hand before the buzzer sounded.

CHANGES OF POSSESSION, INBOUNDING, AND SUSPENSION OF PLAY

After a field goal, the nonscoring team is awarded possession of the ball (sometimes referred to simply as *possession*). The ball also changes team possession if: 1) the offensive team commits a rule infraction; 2) a ball handler steps out of bounds (i.e., touches the floor on or beyond the court boundary); or 3) the ball goes out of bounds after last touching an offensive player, or touches an offensive player who is standing out of bounds (the ball is not considered out of bounds unless it touches the floor on or beyond the court boundary, or touches a player standing out of bounds).

In any of these situations, play stops momentarily, and the new offensive team is given an opportunity to *inbound* the ball—that is, to resume play by passing the ball from out of bounds to a player standing in bounds. Such a pass is called an *inbounds pass* (or *throw-in*), and can be intercepted by the opposing team. What's more, it must be thrown within five seconds of the time the inbounding passer takes possession of the ball, or else the opposing team is awarded an opportunity to inbound the ball. Failure to inbound the ball within five seconds is called a *five-second violation*.

Inbounding the ball is the usual method of resuming play, which stops whenever: 1) a field goal is scored; 2) a rule infraction is committed by either team (defensive infractions will be discussed shortly); 3) a player in possession of the ball steps out of bounds; 4) the ball itself goes out of bounds; or 5) a period ends. If the ball goes out of bounds after last touching a defender, or touches a defender who is standing out of bounds, the offensive team retains possession of the ball, with an opportunity to inbound it. An inbounds pass ordinarily is thrown from a spot close to the occurrence that warranted it. After a field goal, the ball is inbounded from anywhere behind the nearest end line. An official must handle the ball before any inbounds pass except one that follows a field goal—which insures a degree of readiness on the part of the defending team.

THE BASKET, THE BACKBOARD, AND REBOUNDS

The basket ring is attached to the backboard one foot above its bottom edge by a six-inch-long metal flange that is considered part of the basket (see illustration 4). The basket ring itself is sometimes called the *rim*, or *basket rim*. From it hangs a white cord *net* fifteen to eighteen inches in length, which is designed to slow the ball momentarily as it passes through the hoop, thus making it easy to determine whether or not a shot has been successful. The white outline of a rectangle eighteen inches high and twenty-four inches wide (see illustration 3) is centered on the backboard behind the basket to give shooters a point of reference, since many shots are intended to carom off the backboard and into the hoop. A small red light mounted behind the backboard lights up when the buzzer sounds to indicate the end of a period (and may also light up whenever the game clock stops).

All surfaces of the backboard, including its edges, are considered in bounds, except for its back surface.

An errant shot that bounces back toward the court from off the basket or an inbounds surface of the backboard is called a *rebound*. Catching a rebound is known as *rebounding* and is a very important part of basketball, because the rebounding player gains possession of the ball. The tallest players have a distinct rebounding advantage because the ball descends from basket level, which is ten feet above the floor (see illustration 8). In the absence of a rule infraction, play continues uninterrupted on a rebound unless the ball bounces directly over the top of the backboard and passes through the board's plane as it heads toward the end line—in which case the ball is considered to have gone out of bounds.

GOALTENDING AND OFFENSIVE INTERFERENCE

A defender is only permitted to block an opponent's shot while the ball is ascending, or while it is at the apex of its ascent. Once a shot begins to descend, the ball cannot be touched by a defender until it has passed below basket level (unless the shot is obviously so wide off the mark as to have no chance of success to begin with). Nor is a defender permitted (on a shot) to touch the ball after it has hit the backboard (while it still has a chance to carom into the basket); nor to trap the ball between his hand or arm and the backboard; nor to interfere with the ball or basket while the ball is touching the basket; nor to touch the ball while it is anywhere within an imaginary cylinder extending upward from the basket rim. A violation of any of these rules is called *goaltending*, and a shot on which there is a goaltending violation is counted as a field goal—regardless of whether or not the ball actually passes through the hoop.

It is also against the rules for an offensive player to interfere with the ball or basket while the ball is touching the basket or is anywhere directly above the basket in the previously described imaginary cylinder. Such a violation is called *offensive interference* (or simply *interference*), and nullifies any resulting field goal in addition to awarding the ball to the defensive team.

PERSONAL FOULS

As was previously mentioned, it is against the rules for any player to hold, push, strike, or trip an opponent, or to impede his progress by extending the arms. Such an infraction is called a *personal foul* (or *foul*, or *personal*). If an official determines that a foul has been committed, he blows his whistle to stop play, raising his fist to indicate the foul, and identifies the guilty player (who is said to have *fouled* the victim) as well as the manner in which the foul occurred.

A player is allowed to commit a maximum of five personal fouls per game. If he commits a sixth personal, he *fouls out* (or is *disqualified*)—that is, he must leave the game, without option of returning, and must be replaced by a substitute. For this reason, a running tally of the total number of personal fouls each player commits during a game is closely monitored.

A personal foul committed by an offensive player is called an *offensive foul*—unless it occurs while the ball is *loose* (i.e., in no player's possession, as when a shot or rebound is in flight), in which case it is considered a *loose ball foul*, which will be discussed shortly. An offensive foul awards the ball to the other team and, if committed by a shooter as he makes a field goal, nullifies the field goal. Fouls are often further identified by the manner in which they occurred. For example, *charging* is a common offensive foul in which a dribbler runs, or charges, into a defender who has already established a fixed position in front of him. If the defender did not establish his position in front of the dribbler, but instead moved into his path as the contact was made, a foul is called on the defender. Such a foul is known as *blocking*, as is any foul that involves impeding the progress of an opponent.

Because of the nature of a defender's task, defensive fouls (personal fouls committed by defenders) occur much more frequently than do offensive fouls. A defender trying to block a shot or make a steal might easily strike his opponent inadvertently on the wrist, for example, or nudge the shooter's body with his hip—thus committing a personal foul. The ultimate penalty for a defensive foul is the awarding of special penalty shots—which are called *free throws*, or *foul shots*, and will be described shortly—to the player who was fouled. However, not every defensive foul awards a free throw to the fouled player.

If a player commits any personal foul other than an offensive foul, his team is charged with a *team foul* (except in the unlikely event of a *double foul*—two simultaneous fouls committed by opposing players against one another—in which case the personal fouls are not added to team foul totals). A team's fifth team foul in a quarter (or its fourth team foul in an overtime period) puts that team *over the limit*—that is, over an established limit of four team fouls in a quarter (or three in an overtime period). A team that is over the limit incurs a penalty for the remainder of the period, during which that team is said to be in a *penalty situation*. Ordinarily, if a defender fouls an opponent who is not in the act of shooting, no free throw is awarded; play stops; the guilty player is assessed a personal foul; his team is charged with a team foul; and the other team inbounds the ball (from a sideline point at least nineteen feet from the end line) to resume play. However, if such a foul is committed by a defender whose team is in a penalty situation, the player who was fouled is awarded two successive free throws.

A team that has not yet gone over the limit is permitted a maximum of one team foul in the last two minutes of a period, and enters a penalty situation on its second such foul in that interval. Teams are notified that there are two minutes remaining in a period by a public-address announcement.

Regardless of any penalty situation, whenever a defender fouls an opponent who is in the act of shooting, the fouled player is awarded at least one free throw. A player who is fouled while taking an unsuccessful shot is awarded two free throws; one who is fouled while making a field goal is awarded a single free throw. (Normally, a field goal does not count if the shooter was fouled before the shot was taken; however, if the field goal resulted from a continuous motion which started before the foul occurred, a *continuation* is ruled—which means that the field goal counts, even though the foul occurred before the shot.)

If a player on either team commits a loose ball foul (i.e., a foul occurring when the ball is loose), he is charged with a personal foul, his team is charged with a team foul, and the opposing team inbounds the ball—unless the fouling team is in a penalty situation (in which case two shots are awarded), or unless the foul is committed by a defensive player and occurs while a successful shot is in flight (in which case the field goal counts and the fouled player is awarded one free throw). During the last two minutes of a game or overtime period, if a defender commits a deliberate personal foul *off the ball* (that is, away from the ball), the fouled player gets one free throw and his team retains possession of the ball with an inbounds pass.

Alongside the court is a table known as the *scorer's table*, where the *official scorer* (who compiles the official statistics of the game) and *timers* (who operate the game clock and another clock to be described shortly) sit. Whenever a personal foul is called, someone at this table holds up a small red paddle marked by a number indicating how many personal fouls the guilty player has committed thus far in the game. If the foul is a team foul as well, a white paddle is also held up to indicate the number of team fouls committed by the fouling team so far in the period.

TECHNICAL FOULS

In addition to personal fouls and team fouls, there is a third kind of foul, called a *technical foul* (or *technical*, or "*T*"). A technical foul counts as neither a personal nor a team foul, and is normally assessed for unsportsmanlike conduct—such as showing disrespect to an official or flagrantly displaying anger at an official's call. However, technical fouls are also assessed for certain other rule infractions, such as grabbing and hanging onto the basket rim.

A technical foul awards one free throw to the opposing team, which can choose the shooter from among

A Spectator's Guide to Basketball

its five on-court players. After such a free throw, the shooting team retains possession of the ball with an inbounds pass. A technical foul can be called on any player or substitute, as well as on any *coach*. On his second technical foul in a game, a player or coach is *ejected*—that is, he must leave the court and adjacent area for the game's duration.

FREE THROWS AND THE LANE

As was previously stated, free throws are special penalty shots. They differ from field-goal attempts in several ways. First, free throws are taken when play has been suspended, and no defender is allowed to impede or otherwise interfere with the ball or the free-throw shooter. Second, free throws must be shot from behind the *free-throw line* (or *foul line*, or simply the *line*)—a sixteen-foot-long line centered in front of each basket and running parallel to the baseline at a distance of nineteen feet (see illustration 1). Third, a successful free throw is worth only one point to the shooting team. To distinguish them from free throws, field-goal attempts are sometimes referred to as shots taken *from the field* (or *from the floor*)—meaning that they are taken during play. (Note: a field-goal attempt that happens to be taken from the foul line is not considered a free throw, and scores the normal two points if successful.)

A player shooting a free throw (see illustration 9) is often described as being *at the free-throw line* (or *at the foul line*, or simply *at the line*)—because free-throw shooters (or *foul shooters*) stand as close to the line as they legally can, to minimize their distance from the basket. Because free throws are undefended they are relatively easy to make, and a good foul shooter will succeed on 80 percent or more of his attempts. On the final free throw awarded for a given foul, play resumes as soon as the ball leaves the shooter's hands. If the shot misses both backboard and basket, the nonshooting team inbounds the ball from the end line.

Two lines running perpendicular to the free-throw line extend from its ends to the baseline, forming a rectangle nineteen feet long and sixteen feet wide (see illustration 1). This rectangle encloses a painted area variously known as the *lane*, *free-throw lane*, *foul lane*, *three-second lane* (for reasons to be explained shortly), *paint*, or *paint area*.

Along each side of the lane, on its outside, is a series of marks called *lane-space marks*, whose purpose is to indicate where the players (other than the free-throw shooter) can legally stand during a free throw, in anticipation of a rebound (see illustration 9). The rules governing the position of these players are as follows: 1) Players must either stand in the *lane spaces* (the spaces between the lane-space marks), one player to a space, or they must stand away from the lane, at least six feet from the shooter. 2) On each side of the lane, a defender must stand between the baseline and first lane-space mark, and an offensive player must stand in the next available space. 3) It is not mandatory for a defender to occupy the third lane space on either side, though no offensive player is permitted in these spaces. 4) A total of no more than three defenders and two offensive players can occupy the lane spaces before the free throw is released. 5) The free-throw shooter cannot enter the lane until the ball touches the basket or backboard. 6) The other players must remain outside the lane until the ball leaves the free-throw shooter's hand.

A violation of any of the above-mentioned rules is called a *free-throw violation*. (It may also be called a *lane violation* if it involves prematurely entering the lane.) A free-throw violation committed by a defender awards an extra free throw if the shot on which the violation occurred was unsuccessful, and is disregarded if the shot was successful. A free-throw violation on the part of an offensive player nullifies any point scored on the shot, and awards the ball to the opposing team.

When a player's team has possession of the ball during game action, he can legally remain in his own lane (the lane by his own basket) no longer than three seconds at a time without the ball being shot. This is an important rule in basketball, and its violation—known as a *three-second violation* (or simply *three seconds*)— awards the ball to the other team.

JUMP BALLS

During game action the ball is said to be *in play*. Hence, resuming or commencing play is known as *putting the ball in play*. There are only three ways to put the ball in play in basketball. As was previously mentioned, the usual method is an inbounds pass, though play may also resume on a missed free throw.

The third method of putting the ball in play is called a *jump ball* and involves two opposing players vying to tap the ball with a hand to their teammates as it is tossed into the air by an official (see illustrations 7 and 10). These two players jump vertically in their efforts to tap the ball; hence the term "jump ball."

Jump balls are used in situations where possession of the ball is undecided or in dispute. They may take place in either of two circles, called *foul circles* (or *free-throw circles*), which are twelve feet in diameter and are bisected by the foul lines; or they may take place at *center court* (the court's very center), in a circle four feet in diameter called the *jump circle* or *tip-off circle*, which is concentric with a larger circle twelve feet in diameter called the *restraining circle* (see illustration 1). However, all jump balls are governed by the same rules.

The game begins with a jump ball at center court called the *opening jump* (or *opening tap*, or *opening tip*, or *opening tip-off*, or *tip-off*), for which each team can select its jumper (i.e., the one who vies to tap the ball) from among its five players. Given such a choice, a team will usually select one of its tallest men (though it may instead choose one whose leaping ability enables him to out-reach taller teammates). Before the ball is tossed into the air by the official, the jumpers must have at least one foot within that half of the jump circle closest to their own basket, and they cannot move laterally from the circle until the ball is tapped. What's more, they cannot touch the ball until it has reached its apex, cannot tap it more than twice, and cannot gain its possession until it has first touched either the court floor (in bounds), the basket, the backboard, or one of the other eight players. Until the ball is tapped, these eight players must remain outside the restraining circle. (On a jump ball that does not take place at center court, the free-throw circle functions as a restraining circle enclosing an imaginary jump circle.) If a violation of any of the above-mentioned rules benefits the guilty team, the opposing team gets to inbound the ball—if neither jumper manages to tap the tossed ball, the jump ball is repeated.

The team that wins the opening jump (that is, the team that gains possession of the ball as a result of the jump) inbounds the ball from the end line farthest from its basket to begin the fourth period. The other team (the one that lost the opening jump) inbounds the ball to begin the second and third quarters. A similar jump ball at center court also begins all overtime periods.

A jump ball at center court also puts the ball in play if there is a double foul "on the ball" (i.e., involving a player in possession of the ball, or about to catch it); however, in this case the jumpers can't be chosen by the teams, but must be the two foulers. (In the case of a double foul off the ball, the offensive team retains possession with an inbounds pass—unless the fouls occur while an unsuccessful field-goal attempt is in flight, in which case a jump ball takes place at the nearest free-throw circle.)

In addition, a jump ball resumes play if: 1) the ball becomes lodged between the backboard and the basket (in which case each team can choose its jumper); 2) the ball goes out of bounds after last touching two opposing players simultaneously (in which case those two players must jump); 3) two opponents gain simultaneous possession of the ball (in which case those two players must jump); or 4) two opponents commit simultaneous free-throw violations (in which case each team can choose its jumper). In any of these four situations (all of which involve a suspension of play), the jump ball takes place either at center court or in a free-throw circle—whichever of the three locations is closest to the occurrence warranting the jump ball.

THE SHOT CLOCK AND THE 24-SECOND RULE

Once a team gains possession of the ball, that team has twenty-four seconds in which to shoot. If a team fails to shoot within its allotted twenty-four seconds, the ball is awarded to the other team. (To count as a shot in this context, the ball must touch either the basket or the backboard.) If a team rebounds its own missed shot, it gets another twenty-four seconds in which to shoot again, and so on.

The time remaining within the offensive team's allotted 24-second span is displayed on a special digital clock called the *shot clock* (or *24-second clock*), which is located where the players and spectators can easily see it. (There are usually several such clocks positioned around the court.) The shot clock is reset to twenty-four seconds whenever the ball changes team possession, and only runs when the ball is in play. For example, if a defender knocks the ball out of bounds with, say, seventeen seconds remaining on the shot clock, it stops momentarily (because play stops whenever the ball goes out of bounds), and restarts with seventeen seconds still remaining when the ball is inbounded. However, if the ball goes out of bounds after last touching a defender, and with less than five seconds left on the shot clock, it is reset to five seconds (to give the offensive team a reasonable chance to shoot) before starting again on the inbounds pass.

THE 10-SECOND RULE AND BACK-COURT VIOLATIONS

A line known as the *division line* (or *midcourt line*; often referred to simply as *midcourt*) runs from sideline to sideline through the very middle of the court, dividing it into two *half-courts* (see illustration 1). That half of the court farthest from a team's basket is called that team's *back court*, and the other half of the court is called its *front court*. The division line is sometimes referred to as the *timeline*, or *10-second line*, because a team that inbounds the ball in its own back court (for example, following an opponent's field goal) has ten seconds in which to advance the ball into its front court. Failure to advance the ball across the division line within ten seconds awards the ball to the other team, and is known as a *10-second violation*.

Once a team has possession of the ball in its own front court, its players are not permitted to dribble, pass, or knock the ball into the back court, nor can they step on or across the division line while handling the ball. An infraction of this kind is called a *back-court violation* (or simply *back court*), and awards the ball to the other team.

TIMING THE GAME

The game clock starts on the opening jump. From that point on, it stops whenever play stops, with one exception: the clock normally keeps running after a field goal, even though play momentarily stops. However, during the final two minutes of the fourth quarter and of any overtime period, the clock stops whenever a field goal is scored. An official blows his whistle to stop the clock in a jump-ball situation, as well as on a foul or a *violation* (any rule infraction other than a foul—including a ball handler or the ball going out of bounds).

An inactive game clock begins running whenever the ball is put in play. In the case of an inbounds pass, the clock starts when the ball first touches a player in bounds. On a jump ball, the clock starts when the ball is legally tapped. When the last free throw awarded for a given foul is unsuccessful, the clock starts as soon as the rebound touches a player (or as soon as the ball is inbounded, if the shot misses both basket and backboard).

TIMEOUTS

If a team in possession of the ball wishes to stop play (and the clock) for a short interval, it can do so by signaling its intention to an official. Such a pause is called a *timeout* and is normally requested (or *called*) in order to plan strategy, as well as to strategically stop the clock with time about to run out in a period. A team calls a timeout (or *calls time*) by having one of its five players form a "T" with his arms. (Note: when made by an official, this signal indicates a technical foul.)

There are two kinds of timeouts: a *regular timeout*, which lasts ninety seconds, and a *20-second timeout*. Each team is permitted no more than one 20-second timeout per half. A team must take at least one regular timeout per period, and is limited to no more than seven in a *regulation-length* game (a game that ends after the usual four quarters, without any overtime). A team is also limited to no more than four regular timeouts in the fourth period, and no more than three in the last two minutes of the fourth period. In any overtime period, each team is permitted no more than two regular timeouts.

SUBSTITUTIONS

Player substitutions cannot be made while the clock is running. They can be made whenever the clock is stopped, with one exception: a substitute cannot enter the game following a field goal unless a technical foul has been called. Before coming onto the court, a substitute must first enter a rectangular area in front of the scorer's table to notify the official scorer of the substitution—which is signalled by the sounding of a horn or buzzer when play has stopped (unless the substitution takes place between periods). A player who has been replaced by another can return to the game, and there is no limit on the number of times a player can enter and leave the game.

COACHES

A team's coaching staff consists of a *head coach* and one or two *assistant coaches*. During play, the coaches and those players not currently in the game sit along one sideline, just out of bounds. As he shouts instructions to his players during game action, a coach is not permitted to come onto the court, but can leave his seat and pace along the sideline from the nearest baseline to a sideline *hash mark* (short on-court mark) twenty-eight feet from that baseline (see illustration 1).

UNIFORMS

Players wear sneakers plus uniforms consisting of shorts and sleeveless shirts (see illustration 5). For ease of identification, each player on a team is assigned his own number, which is displayed on his shirt along with his surname and the name of his team. When an official calls a foul, he indicates the guilty player's uniform number by holding up the appropriate number of fingers. (For example, he holds up four fingers on each hand to indicate that the foul was committed by player number forty-four.) Teams wear light-colored uniforms while playing at home, and dark ones while playing on the road.

OFFICIALS' SIGNALS

The officials identify their calls with special hand signals. For instance, to indicate the team that is to get possession of the ball, an official points in that team's offensive direction and calls out the team's uniform color; and to call a jump ball, he raises both arms in the air with his thumbs up. To cancel a field goal or free throw (or a sequence of action) because of an infraction, he crosses his arms in front of him (with palms down) and then sweeps them outward. To indicate that a field goal counts despite a foul, he makes a downward-sweeping motion with his arm. During play, he raises one arm to indicate that a shot was taken from beyond the three-point line, and raises the other arm as well if the shot is successful. It is not essential for a fan to learn the other signals used by the officials, as the calls involved are explained over a loudspeaker by a courtside announcer (as well as by many radio and TV broadcasters).

CHAPTER 2
Offense

PLAYER POSITIONS

Each of the five players on a basketball team has a particular *position* to play. A player's position is a "job title" of sorts, related to his on-court role, his style of play, and his size (which helps determine his role and style of play). There are three basic positions in basketball: *center*, *forward*, and *guard*.

The center is normally the tallest of the five players, followed by the forwards and finally the guards—who, while usually the smallest players on the court, are still quite tall compared to the average person. In the NBA and major college basketball, most centers are somewhere around seven feet tall, and some are seven feet plus; while very few guards are under six feet, and most are taller. Forwards tend to be somewhere in between. However, exceptions are common: for example, the guard who stands six feet eight, or the forward who is taller than his team's center.

Though all five players handle the ball, shoot, and constantly move all over the court, there are certain general offensive tendencies that help distinguish guards, forwards, and centers from one another. For instance, although size is an advantage in rebounding, it is a disadvantage in dribbling—because the taller the dribbler, the farther the ball has to travel from the floor to his hand. Thus while a team's guards are usually its least effective rebounders, they are always its best dribblers, and dribble more than do forwards and centers. As part of their dribbling chores, guards are charged with the duty of dribbling the ball *upcourt* (that is, toward the other end of the court; also known as *downcourt*) after it has been inbounded in the back court. Once the ball is in their front court, the guards tend to stay *outside* (that is, some distance from the basket)—except when *driving* (dribbling while running toward the basket, or near it, for a shot or quick pass to a teammate).

The two guards on a team are collectively referred to as that team's *back court* (not to be confused with the part of the court called the back court). There are actually two basic types of guard: the *point guard* and the *shooting guard* (sometimes called the *off guard*, or *big guard*). These two types usually—but not necessarily—play in tandem. The point guard is an expert dribbler, and does more dribbling than the shooting guard; thus, he is normally the one to bring the ball upcourt. The point guard must also be a skilled passer, because one of his primary offensive functions is to pass the ball to teammates who are *open* (i.e., who are within shooting range and sufficiently free of defenders to take an unimpeded shot). Most point guards are also adept at *penetrating* (that is, driving to the basket through the defenders) which requires that they be quick-moving. Because the shortest players are generally the quickest-moving as well as the best dribblers, point guards tend to be the shortest players in the game. Because they handle the ball so much, they tend to control and direct the offensive flow of the game—another of the point guard's major functions. The point guard is sometimes called the *playmaker* (or *play-

making guard)—"playmaker" referring to a player who passes and dribbles the ball in such a way as to create open (i.e., unimpeded) shots for his teammates.

The shooting guard does less dribbling than does the point guard, though he must still be a reasonably skilled dribbler. He is usually taller than the point guard, and as might be guessed from his name, his main offensive function is to shoot the ball—often from the outside. Thus a shooting guard should have a good outside shot (i.e., he should be adept at scoring field goals from the outside).

Because they are normally taller than the guards, forwards are generally not as skillful at dribbling—though they are usually more effective rebounders. When their team has the ball in the front court, the forwards tend to stay *inside*—that is, somewhere close to the basket, from where many of their shots are taken. In order to help create wide spaces between the defenders, each of whom normally defends against one particular opponent throughout the game (see Chapter 3), forwards may also move to the *corners* (that is, somewhere near the corners formed by the baseline and sidelines)—and are thus sometimes known as *cornermen*. Wide spaces between defenders provide the offensive players with room to maneuver and drive to the hoop.

There are two types of forward: the *small forward* and the *power forward* (sometimes called the *big forward*, or *strong forward*). These two types usually—but not necessarily—play in tandem. As his name suggests, the small forward is the smaller of the two. He is quicker-moving and a better dribbler than the power forward, and is thus more apt to drive with the ball. The power forward, as might be expected, is a more effective rebounder.

The center is normally the tallest of the five players on a basketball team. Consequently he is usually the best rebounder—and the clumsiest dribbler. When his team has the ball in its own front court, the center often stations himself either *high* (i.e., near the foul line; also known as *up high*) or *low* (i.e., close to the basket; also known as *down low*). A team's center and two forwards are referred to collectively as that team's *front line*.

SHOOTING

Shooting is the essence of basketball offense, and is done on the move or standing still, depending on the situation. There are several different types of shots. One of the easiest to make is the *layup* (or *lay-in*), which involves *laying the ball up*—that is, throwing the ball gently into the basket from almost directly underneath (see illustration 11). A layup is usually taken as the shooter drives to the basket, and is often *banked* (i.e., bounced off the backboard) into the hoop. Players seldom miss layups because they are taken from such close range.

Another sure shot is the dunk—which, as previously mentioned, involves throwing the ball down through the basket from directly above it (see illustration 12). However, in order to reach high enough to dunk the ball, a player must be either very tall or a very high leaper.

The most common shot in basketball is the *jump shot*, or *jumper*, in which the shooter leaves his feet and releases the ball with arms raised while at the apex of his jump (see illustration 13). The main rationale behind such a maneuver is that it makes the shot more difficult to block than if the ball were released while the shooter was standing on the ground. The jump shot is a versatile shot that can be taken from virtually anywhere within a shooter's normal shooting range—which in some cases extends beyond the three-point line.

A fourth type of shot is the *hook shot*, or *hook*, in which the shooter pivots on the foot opposite his shooting hand and, with his body turned sideways to the basket, releases the ball with a hooking, upward-sweeping motion of the arm farthest from the basket (see illustration 14). The hook shot is difficult to block because the ball is protected from the defender by the shooter's body. However, the accuracy of such a shot is somewhat limited, and thus it is normally taken from fairly close to the basket.

Shots are often described in terms of the shooter's

distance from the basket (measured from a point on the floor directly under the hoop). For example, a fifteen-foot shot (or "fifteen-footer") is one that's taken by a player who is fifteen feet from a point on the floor directly under the basket.

There are great differences between individual players with regard to shooting range. For instance, some shooters have difficulty with outside shots, and thus rarely take one; while others are fairly accurate even from several feet beyond the three-point line. But regardless of the shooter, the closer to the basket he is as he releases the ball, the easier the shot usually is.

OFFENSIVE TACTICS

The main idea of basketball offense is to take the easiest shot possible—and to make sure the shot is not blocked by a defender. One means of doing this is by *screening* (or *picking*). Screening involves an offensive player without the ball positioning himself in such a way as to obstruct an opponent from reaching and defending against the shooter (see illustration 15). The obstruction itself is called a *screen*, or *pick*, and is said to have been *set* by the screening player—who must be stationary or moving in the same direction and path as his opponent, and who cannot dart into the path of a moving opponent at the last second to precipitate a collision. The obstructed defender—who may or may not inadvertently run into the screener—is said to have been *picked off*, or *screened*. Screens are an important part of the game, but are easily overlooked by the spectator, who tends to focus on the ball handler rather than the other players.

Another commonly used tactic for setting up open, easy shots involves players *cutting* (that is, running without the ball in the area around the basket) so that they can break free of defenders and receive a pass. To elude defenders, a cutting player will often make a false start in one direction before running the other way, and may also make frequent, unexpected changes in direction.

Because offensive players are constantly cutting, a

ball handler who is not intent on shooting should always be on the alert for open teammates so that he can pass the ball to them for a quick shot before a defender arrives. However, sometimes it is the passer himself who creates open shots by attracting several defenders as he penetrates to the basket, and then throwing the ball to a teammate who has been left *unguarded* (i.e., unattended by a defender). Such a maneuver is a favorite ploy of many point guards, and depends for its success on the fact that a penetrator is likely to shoot an easy layup if left alone.

As the only means of getting the ball to an open teammate, passing is a crucial ingredient to offensive success. A pass that leads directly to a field goal by the recipient is called an *assist*. Not surprisingly, point guards—for whom passing is a major function—tend to make more assists than do their teammates.

Still another common offensive tactic is to try and create *mismatches*. A mismatch involves the isolation of the shooter against either a much smaller defender down low, or a much slower defender outside. (The taller a player is, the slower he usually is; so outside mismatches usually involve taller defenders.) Normally each defender *guards* (i.e., defends against) one particular opponent throughout the game and tries to stay close to him even when he doesn't have the ball (see Chapter 3). Such a pairing is called a *match-up*, and nearly always involves players of roughly the same size and speed (and thus of the same position). This is because it is difficult for a defender to block the shot of a much taller opponent (since most shots are released with the shooting arm upraised) and to keep up with a much faster opponent. Thus, in a mismatch, a taller ball handler down low may score an easy field goal by *shooting over* his opponent (that is, by shooting over the defender's upraised arms, without the shot being blocked), and a quick ball handler positioned outside may drive past his slower opponent for a possible layup. Mismatches usually result from screens, as the shooter's normal defender—obstructed in his efforts to shadow his quarry—is temporarily replaced by a shorter or slower teammate.

PLAYS

The means of coordinating the various offensive tactics and combining them into one coherent plan of attack is the *play*. In its most general sense, a "play" is any sequence of basketball action. However, the term is also used interchangeably with "*set play*," which refers to a planned sequence of offensive maneuvering designed to produce an open, easy shot for one of the players. For simplicity's sake, the term "play" will be used only in the latter sense (i.e., to mean "set play") throughout the rest of this chapter.

Plays involve various combinations of cutting, dribbling, driving, screening, and passing—often giving the action a chaotic appearance. But this semblance of chaos is deceptive: plays are often highly organized, well-rehearsed, disciplined affairs in which each offensive player has his own specific function to carry out (which normally involves either setting a screen, handling the ball, or drawing defenders away from the ball handlers).

Each play is identified by its own special code name and hand signal, and usually has a number of *options*, or alternative courses of action, which are designed to anticipate the various ways in which the defenders might initially react. Usually it is the coach who *calls* the play—that is, who indicates which play to execute (or *run*) by shouting out the code name or giving the hand signal. Often he conveys this information to the point guard, who then relays it to his teammates.

ONE-ON-ONE PLAY

Not every sequence of offensive action that takes place on a basketball court is part of a carefully planned play. At times the offensive strategy is left to the discretion of the individual players, who still may pass, cut, and set screens, but in a more spontaneous fashion.

And sometimes the players don't do much passing, cutting, or screening at all, but instead adopt a more individualistic style. In such an offense, the shooter goes *one-on-one* against his defender—that is, he attempts to score largely by his own efforts against his defender. While a player going one-on-one may dribble past a teammate to use him as a screen, for the most part he relies on his own ability to beat his defender by using a variety of deceptive maneuvers known as *moves*. (In a more general sense, "move" can refer to any offensive maneuver by a dribbler, cutter, or shooter.)

There is almost no limit to the number of possible moves a ball handler may use to break free of his defender and shoot his shot without hindrance. For instance, he may suddenly whirl in another direction as he dribbles the ball, or he may switch the ball to his other hand just before he releases a driving, mid-air shot. Many moves involve *faking*—that is, false movement intended to fool (or *fake out*) a defender. For example, a ball handler might take a false step to his left and then, as his defender follows suit, quickly drive to his right. Another kind of fake is the *double-pump* (or *double-clutch*), in which a leaping player makes a false shooting motion with his arms before finally releasing his shot—thus making it difficult to block.

One-on-one play is not limited to a spontaneous, individualistic style of offensive attack. Sometimes, as part of a set play, the teammates of a particularly skillful one-on-one player may *clear out* a side of the court for him. This involves intentionally vacating one side of the front court to give the shooter maneuvering room as he goes one-on-one against his defender, and to make sure no other defenders stand in his way.

Although one-on-one play can be crowd-pleasing because of the moves it often showcases, a team that relies on it too much is at a disadvantage. Basketball is a team game, and—other things being equal—five players working together as a single unit will score many more points than a collection of five individuals, each acting more or less on his own. This is because teamwork—whose offensive components are passing, cutting, and screening—generally produces much easier shots than those taken by players going one-on-one.

THE FAST BREAK

In addition to passing, screening, cutting, and one-on-one moves, there is another way to get an easy, open shot: the *fast break* (or *break*). A fast break occurs when a team gains possession of the ball in the back court and attempts to bring the ball upcourt at top speed before the defenders can arrive there from their previous offensive positions. Such a tactic is unlikely to succeed when the ball is inbounded, because the short break in action preceding the inbounds pass invariably gives the opposing players sufficient time to take their proper defensive positions. However, the fast break can be very effective when it follows a rebound of the opposing team's shot, which is how the maneuver usually begins.

If a team intends to fast break (that is, if it intends to execute a fast break), it will send one or more of its players *breaking* (running toward their own basket from the back court) as soon as an opponent takes a shot. If the shot misses and is rebounded by a defender (as are most missed shots; see Chapter 3), he will immediately pass the ball far downcourt to one of his breaking teammates. Such a pass is called an *outlet pass*, and is usually caught on the dead run. Sometimes, if the rebounder is a skillful enough dribbler and a fast enough runner, he will start the break himself by dribbling downcourt in an attempt to outrace his opponents.

If no opponent manages to get back downcourt in time to defend against the fast break, it will almost surely result in a successful layup or dunk. But even if a few opponents manage to get back in time, the fast break is likely to produce an easy shot, as long as the breaking players outnumber the ready defenders. Fast breaks are often described in terms of the ratio of breakers to defending opponents. For instance, a "three-on-one break" involves three breaking players facing only one defender.

The offensive players involved in a fast break usually follow certain routes designed to take maximum advantage of their temporary superiority in numbers. These routes generally involve each breaker *filling a lane*—that is, running down either side of the court, or down its middle. Often a teammate called the *trailer* follows a short distance behind to tip in a missed shot or to receive a possible pass if none of the breakers has an open shot.

OFFENSIVE REBOUNDS

The fast break depends on *defensive rebounding*—that is, rebounding of the opposing team's shots—which usually begins the maneuver. However, *offensive rebounding*—that is, a team's rebounding of its own shots—is also an important aspect of offensive play, because it gives the rebounding team another chance to score before giving up possession of the ball. What's more, an offensive rebounder often finds himself with an easy, open shot as a result of his position near the basket. A very effective form of offensive rebounding is the previously mentioned tip-in, in which the rebounder doesn't catch the ball, but merely tips it into the basket for a field goal.

RUNNING OUT THE CLOCK

In sharp distinction to the fast break is the slow, deliberate style of offensive play often employed by a team that gets the ball with around twenty-four seconds (or less) remaining in a period. Unless the game is about to end and the team in question is behind, it will usually *run out the clock* (or *use up the clock*); that is, its players will dribble, pass, and hold the ball for nearly the full twenty-four seconds allowed before shooting, so that the period will end before the other team has another chance to score. A similar offensive tactic may be employed in the last few minutes of a game by a team that is well ahead—the idea being to use up as much official game time as possible while giving the opposing team a minimal number of scoring chances.

TURNOVERS

Regardless of its style of play, the offensive team tries to avoid making *turnovers*. A turnover is any loss of team ball possession without a shot being taken. Such an unwitting loss of the ball may be caused by a steal, an offensive foul, or a violation. A team that commits a turnover is said to have *turned the ball over* to its opponent (or simply to have turned the ball over).

SUBSTITUTIONS

Basketball is a grueling sport that places tremendous physical demands on its players. The considerable amount of running involved in a game—what with the cutting, driving, fast-breaking, and defending—makes it very difficult for a player to play forty-eight minutes of basketball at top speed. For this reason, every team makes at least some use of player substitutions.

Substitutions are decided by a team's coaches, who may replace one player with another for a variety of reasons. Sometimes the coaches make a substitution merely to give a brief rest to a *starting player* (or *starter*)—that is, one of the five players who *start* the game, or represent their team on the court when the game begins. However, frequently a substitute will be sent into the game because the coaches feel that his particular style of play will result in the team playing more effectively.

For example, during a game in which a particular is scoring a great deal, the coaches might replace the player who has been guarding this scorer with a substitute who has better defensive skills. Or if a team is getting *outrebounded* (that is, if it is not getting as many rebounds as the opposing team), the coaches might replace one of the front-line players with a better rebounder. Many teams, in fact, make liberal use of substitutions, frequently giving almost equal *playing time* (that is, time during which a player is actually in a game) to seven, eight, or even nine main players.

CHAPTER 3
Defense

GUARDING AN OPPONENT

Central to basketball defense is the concept of guarding (or *covering*) an opponent (see illustration 16). To guard an opponent is simply to defend against him when his team is on offense—whether or not he himself has the ball. The purpose of guarding an opponent who doesn't have the ball is to prevent him from catching a pass and taking an open shot. The main purpose of guarding a ball handler is to prevent him from making a field goal—which necessitates blocking his path to the basket and impeding any shot attempt. A defender also tries to block any pass a ball handler might throw. In addition, any defender is always interested in making a steal or otherwise causing a turnover. At the same time, he must be careful not to be overly aggressive, lest he foul the player he is guarding.

Guarding an opponent normally involves staying between him and his basket. However, when the opponent is down low awaiting a pass from outside, his defender may instead *front* him—that is, the defender may stand between the opponent in question and the ball handler, in an effort to discourage or intercept such a pass.

MAN-TO-MAN AND ZONE DEFENSE

There are two main styles of defense in basketball. The first is called *man-to-man defense* (or simply *man-to-man*; sometimes referred to as *man-for-man*), and involves each defender guarding one particular opponent—who is known as that defender's *man*—throughout the game. (The defender is known as his opponent's man, as well.) A defender usually tries to closely follow his man wherever he goes, whether or not he has the ball—unless he strays out of shooting range.

The second type of defense is called *zone defense* (or simply *zone*), and involves each defender patrolling a particular area (or *zone*) of the opposing team's front court, and guarding any opponent who enters that area. Zone defense is illegal in the NBA, but is permitted (and quite common) in college basketball; thus it will be discussed more fully in Chapter 4.

SWITCHING

Despite its individual assignments, basketball defense is not a solitary task in which each defender merely guards his own man (or zone). Rather, defense is a cooperative affair and, to be maximally effective, must involve the same degree of teamwork that characterizes a successful offense. For instance, to cope with the frequent screens set by the offensive team, the defenders use a tactic called *switching*. Switching involves a screened defender temporarily exchanging defensive assignments with a teammate who is in a better position to guard the screened defender's man. Such a maneuver—like many others—depend on verbal signaling between defenders.

DOUBLETEAMING

Another tactic that illustrates the cooperative nature of defense is called *doubleteaming*. Doubleteaming involves two defenders temporarily guarding the same opponent—normally a particularly skillful scorer, who may or may not have the ball. One of the defenders *falls off* his own man (i.e., temporarily leaves the player he is guarding) and comes over to help his teammate guard the player in question. The advantage of doubleteaming is that two defenders are much more effective than one, but the risk is that it leaves one player unguarded.

In the NBA there is a restriction on doubleteaming which hinges on the distinction between two sides of the front court: the *strong side* and the *weak side*. The strong side is that side of the front court on which the ball is at any given moment during game action, and the weak side is the other side. It is illegal for a defender whose own man is on the weak side to doubleteam any opponent who does not have the ball, though these restrictions don't apply to that part of the front court *above* the foul circle (i.e., beyond the foul circle, in a direction toward midcourt).

HELPING OUT

Defensive teamwork requires that defenders assist one another in every way possible throughout the game, a practice known as helping out. One common form involves a defender falling off his own man to help cover a driving opponent who has beaten his defender (that is, who has managed to elude his defender, even if only by a step) and is threatening to score. In such a situation, the center is the ideal defender to help out because, as the tallest player, he is apt to be the best shot-blocker (height being an obvious advantage in shot blocking). Consequently the center's preferred defensive position is usually in the *middle* (the area in front of the basket), because from there he can most readily block the shot of an opponent who drives to the hoop.

Often the mere presence of the defensive center in the middle is enough to discourage opponents from trying to penetrate, because of the shot-blocking threat he poses.

However, because of the ban against zone defense, a defender in the NBA is not allowed to patrol the middle (or any other area of the front court) unless his own man is nearby. What's more, defenders have a lane restriction similar to, but not quite as strict as, that which applies to the offensive team. This defensive lane restriction makes use of the difference in width between the NBA lane (which is sixteen feet across) and the twelve-foot-wide lane used in college basketball (see Chapter 4). The side boundaries of both the college and NBA lanes are marked on every NBA court (see illustration 1), with the narrower college portion of the lane being called the *inside lane* and the rest of the lane, the *outside lane*. (This distinction is made for defensive purposes only; the offensive lane restriction involves the entire NBA lane, to which the term "lane" itself always refers.) While there is no restriction as to how long a defender may remain in the outside lane, a defender cannot remain in the inside lane for longer than 2.9 seconds at a time unless his man is standing within three feet of the lane area (a distance indicated on each side by short hash marks extending from the baseline; see illustration 1).

CONTESTING FOR POSITION

Despite these restrictions, defensive centers in the NBA do in fact tend to stay near the middle, because their offensive counterparts (whom they usually guard) often play down low. However, in addition to helping out against driving opponents, a defensive center is concerned with guarding his own man, who is likely to be quite adept at scoring from near the basket. Consequently, the defensive center tries to prevent his opponent from stationing himself at such an advantageous spot, by occupying that spot himself and forcing his man to stand farther from the basket. The offensive center, for his part, contests this, with the result that the two opposing centers jockey for *position*—that is, they each try to gain the advantage with regard to floor position close to the basket. Such a battle is usually attended by a certain degree of pushing and shoving, which is allowed up to a point. However, such physical contact is only permitted off the ball, never between a defender and the ball handler.

REBOUNDING

Jockeying for position near the basket is not limited to centers, but can involve any offensive player and his defender (though it seldom involves guards, who tend to remain outside on offense). What's more, the position being fought for does not just concern scoring—it often concerns rebounding as well. Rebounding success depends to a large extent on being in the right place to catch the ball as it descends, following a missed shot; and thus opposing players—particularly centers and forwards—normally vie with one another for the best rebounding position.

One form of this jockeying for rebounding position is called *boxing out* (or *blocking out*). Boxing out involves a player facing the basket in anticipation of a rebound and interposing his body between an opponent and the area in front of him where the rebound is expected to fall (see illustration 17). A player may box out an opponent so that he himself can get the rebound, or he may box out so that a teammate may rebound unmolested.

The defensive team has a distinct rebounding advantage over the offensive team. There are three reasons for this: first, defenders normally stand between their men and the basket, thus putting the defenders in better rebounding position; second, many rebounds fall toward the lane, and defenders have less of a lane restriction than do their opponents; and third, offensive players can't afford to be too involved with rebounding or they won't be able to get back downcourt quickly enough to defend against a possible fast break. Consequently the majority of rebounds—though by no

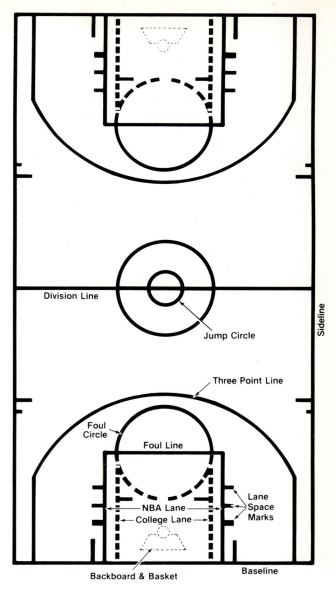

1. Diagram of a basketball court.

2. A basketball.

3. A basket and backboard.

4. Side view of basket, backboard, and supporting base.

5. A player dribbling the ball.

6. A defender blocking an opponent's shot.

7. An official about to toss the ball into the air for a jump ball.

8. Four players vying for a rebound.

9. A player shooting a free throw.

10. A jump ball in progress. The two jumpers are vying to tap the ball, which has been tossed into the air by an official.

11. A player shooting a layup.

12. A player dunking the ball.

13. A player shooting a jump shot.

14. A player shooting a hook shot.

15. The defender on the right is screened by a much larger opponent.

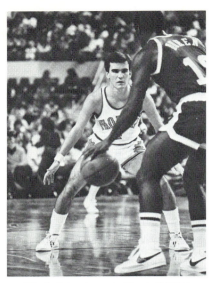

16. A defender guarding a dribbler.

17. As they await a rebound, the player on the left boxes out his opponent.

means all of them—fall into the hands of the defensive team. This is especially true on free throws, because with a player occupying the lane space closest to the basket on each side, the defenders have by far the best rebounding position.

THE PRESS

In its efforts to prevent the opposing team from scoring, the defensive team will occasionally resort to a tactic known as the *press*, which involves unusually close guarding of all five offensive players. Normally a defender won't bother to guard an opponent who is out of shooting range, because guarding him is very tiring and a player out of shooting range does not pose a scoring threat. The press, however, takes a more aggressive approach to defense.

There are two basic types of press: the *full-court press* and the *half-court press*. In a full-court press, the defenders guard their opponents closely from the time the ball is inbounded in the back court, while in a half-court press the close guarding does not begin until the offensive players enter their front court. The purpose of the press is to make a steal or otherwise force the offensive team into turning the ball over. While the press may be used to get the ball back quickly by a team that is behind in the score with little time remaining, it is by no means limited to such situations.

A similar pressing tactic is sometimes used on the inbounds pass itself—that is, the defenders closely guard their opponents before the ball is inbounded, in an effort to intercept the inbounds pass or cause a five-second violation.

DRAWING A CHARGE

Another defensive tactic, which is occasionally employed against a swiftly moving dribbler, is to try and draw a charge—that is, to try and induce the dribbler to commit a charging foul, by establishing position in his path before he has time to change his direction.

This is a risky undertaking, however, because if the defender does not establish his position before the contact is made, he himself is called for the foul.

ILLEGAL DEFENSE

On the court are sideline hash marks twenty-five feet from each baseline, and lane hash marks six feet from each foul line (see illustration 1). These sets of hash marks indicate imaginary cross-court lines which, together with imaginary lines running through the foul lines, divide each front court into four sections for purposes of regulating defensive play. The actual rules involved are complex enough to place them beyond the scope of this book; for the spectator, it is sufficient to know that these four sections figure in the definition of an illegal zone defense.

A violation of the anti-zone rules involving these four front-court sections is called *illegal defense*—as is a violation of the 2.9-second defensive lane limit and the restriction on doubleteaming (both previously described). A team's first illegal-defense violation during a game merely results in an official warning and the shot clock being reset to twenty-four seconds. However, each succeeding illegal-defense violation by that team is considered a technical foul. An illegal-defense violation that occurs during the final twenty-four seconds of any period is considered a technical foul, even if the violation is the team's first in the game.

CHAPTER 4
The Beauty of the Game: Some Things to Look For

Ballet in Sneakers. No other team sport comes close to basketball with regard to the sheer grace of the players' movements, which even the casual fan can appreciate. Basketball is a game in which speed, timing, and finesse reign paramount, and nearly every facet—from dribbling to shooting to shot blocking—reflects this, lending the sport an esthetic appeal that may well be unmatched in the athletic world. As the tall, slender, agile players leap gazellelike through the air in the heat of the fast-paced action, the game seems like some sort of high-speed ballet danced to the rhythms of a bouncing ball.

The Mighty Slam-Dunk. Without a doubt the most crowd-pleasing shot in all of basketball is the slam-dunk, in which the shooter hurls the ball downward through the hoop from directly above, with considerable force. In sharp contrast to all other shots, which depend on a soft and delicate release for their accuracy, the dunk is done with full power, and as such has become the game's supreme gesture of offensive might and defiance—a status helped, too, by the fact that the shooter has managed to get so close to the opposing team's basket. Although it is worth a mere two points, as is any ordinary field goal, the dunk nevertheless lends the shooter a fleeting aura of invincibility. Whether or not the shot is further embellished—as when the ball is dunked backward, from behind the shooter's head, for example—it never fails to impress the typical spectator, for whom a ten-foot-high basket is well out of reach.

The Blocked Shot. The blocked shot is the defensive equivalent of the dunk, both as a purely physical feat and as a symbol of strength and indomitability. It is particularly awe-inspiring when performed by the towering center against a smaller opponent shooting from some distance away—in which case one sees the blocker rise to dizzying heights to swat down a shot that was released with no obstruction in sight. Such an act requires split-second timing as well as quick reactions, and is likely to sound a momentary note of discouragement in the minds of the opposing players, whose subsequent shots may be haunted by visions of long, upraised arms with a seemingly endless reach.

The Fast Break. For sheer excitement, few things in basketball can match the successful fast break, a blitzkreig attack in which several players race downcourt like greyhounds to catch their opponents by surprise and earn an easy field goal. The break combines some of the game's most appealing elements—blazing speed, precision teamwork, and graceful movement—into a few seconds of high drama. With each breaking player following his own route, the ball may never even touch the floor as it's passed in rapid succession from one streaking blur to another to confound the outnumbered defenders—who seem utterly powerless to stop the flying dunk or layup that crowns the whole sequence.

The Skywalkers. Basketball is a game of leaps and bounds, in which shot blocking, rebounding, and even shooting depend, to some degree, on jumping skyward. Some players are able to reach truly prodigious heights, rising more than a yard into the air, as if they had springs in their heels. As they shoot, certain players even appear to defy the laws of gravity by remaining suspended in mid-air for what seems like an extra second before descending, in order to release the ball unimpeded by their more earthbound defenders.

The Phenomenal Accuracy of the Outside Shooter. One of the most impressive displays in basketball involves a dead-eye shooter consistently making shot after shot from long range—say, twenty feet or more from the basket. From that distance, the eighteen-inch-wide hoop looks more the size of a donut, and allows very little margin for error. It's difficult enough to make such a shot with no one in sight; but to do so in the heat of battle, often with a defender's hand waving in the face, requires extraordinary skill and concentration. The sight of the ball soaring in a high, majestic arc to pierce its target without even touching the rim is enough to draw gasps from the crowd—and has an element of added appeal when the shot is taken from three-point range.

Dribbling Wizardry. While it takes no great skill to bounce a ball, it's another matter entirely to do so while running at top speed, frequently changing directions, and keeping a constant eye out for open teammates and defenders looking to make a steal. Such is the task of the point guards, who often put on an incredible show as they whirl, wheel, stop, and start, dribbling behind their backs, between their legs, and every which way, first with one hand and then the other—all the while miraculously controlling the ball, as if it were a yo-yo attached to their fingers by some invisible thread.

The Battle Under the Backboards. While basketball is primarily a sport of speed, finesse, and agility, rebounding is one area in which the tough guys tend to prevail. Although a player's height and the timing of his jump are important in gathering in a missed shot, another critical factor is positioning: a player stationed at the very spot where the rebound descends has the best chance of gaining the ball. The jostling and shoving that occurs beneath the backboards as players—usually the big forwards and centers—vie for good rebounding position is far from gentle, and is followed by equally fierce battling for the ball as they leap high into the air. The power and strength involved in rebounding is never so apparent as when a huge center rises Samson-like from a scattering crowd of smaller players to snag the ball well above basket level.

Driving Assists. A favorite ploy of many point guards is to drive to the basket to attract a horde of defenders and, while still moving at top speed, and pass the ball to a teammate who has been left unguarded. Such a maneuver is as dazzling to spectators as it is frustrating to defenders—especially when, as sometimes happens, the pass recipient is standing behind the passer, who appears for all the world to have eyes in the back of his head.

The Shot at the Buzzer with the Game on the Line. By far the most dramatic moment in basketball occurs when, a split-second before the final buzzer of a very close contest, a player launches an outside shot that can either tie the game or win it for his team. To manage to get such a shot off in time, in the face of the swarming defenders, is an accomplishment in itself; but to keep a steady shooting hand amid such pressure, knowing that the entire game hangs in the balance, requires the proverbial ice water in the veins. The suspense begins building well before the shot is taken, and crescendoes with the sounding of the buzzer, which finds the ball still airborne—and the players and fans watching with their hearts in their mouths.

Body Genius. In no other team sport does a player's creativity have anywhere near the outlet and showcase that is provided by basketball. There is virtually no limit on the possible deceptive moves to which a shooter or dribbler can resort: he might double-pump, switch the ball to the other hand while in mid-air, dribble between his legs or behind his back, whirl 360 degrees on a drive to the hoop, or perform any of a hundred other maneuvers that are equally dazzling—and effective. Such displays of physical artistry—inspired by something for which "body genius" at times seems too mild a term—tend to leave even the seasoned fan in a state of astonished delight.

Teamwork: The Whole Is Greater Than the Sum of Its Parts. Something strange and wondrous seems to happen when the five members of a basketball team manage to play together as a single unit whose only objective is winning—rather than as a collection of five individuals, each with his own dreams of personal glory. On such occasions, the five minds seem to fuse together on some level to form a collective intelligence that operates simultaneously through all five players, coordinating their efforts to an uncanny degree and prompting them to a level of play that none of them as individuals could hope to match. The result is simply basketball at its best—and a rare treat to watch.

CHAPTER 5
The NBA

The NBA, or National Basketball Association, is the major professional basketball league in the United States. It consists of two conferences, each divided into two divisions, as follows:

EASTERN CONFERENCE

Atlantic Division
Boston Celtics
New Jersey Nets (East Rutherford)
New York Knickerbockers
Philadelphia 76ers
Washington Bullets

Central Division
Atlanta Hawks
Chicago Bulls
Cleveland Cavaliers
Detroit Pistons
Indiana Pacers (Indianapolis)
Milwaukee Bucks

A Spectator's Guide to Basketball

WESTERN CONFERENCE

Midwest Division
Dallas Mavericks
Denver Nuggets
Houston Rockets
Kansas City Kings
San Antonio Spurs
Utah Jazz (Salt Lake City)

Pacific Division
Golden State Warriors (Oakland, California)
Los Angeles Lakers
Phoenix Suns
Portland Trail Blazers
San Diego Clippers
Seattle SuperSonics

The official NBA season usually starts around the beginning of November and lasts till mid-April. During this period, each team plays a total of eighty-two games against the other teams in the league. A team plays half of its games at home, and half on the road—with the majority against teams from the same conference.

At the end of the season, the team that has won the most games in its division is declared division champion. Within each conference, the two division champions and the four additional teams that have won the most games enter into post-season *playoff* (i.e., championship tournament) competition to determine the conference champion. The four non-division-winners are ranked from one to four according to total games won during the season, with team one (the team that won the most season games) playing a best-of-three-game series against team four, and team two playing a similar series against team three. ("Best-of-three" means that the first team to win two games is the series winner; "three" refers to the maximum number of games such a series can last.)

The winners of these "*mini-series*" then each play a best-of-seven-game series against one of the two division champions, with the division champion that won the most season games playing either team one or four, and the other division champion playing either team two or three. (In a best-of-seven series, the first team to win four games is the winner.) The winners of these two series then face each other in another best-of-seven series to determine the conference champion. Finally, the two conference champions meet in one last best-of-seven series to determine the NBA champion. This final, championship series usually begins some time in late May.

Any ties for either playoff opportunity, playoff precedence, or division championship are settled by the first applicable method in a series of methods comparing various aspects of team performance during the season—beginning with the tied teams' success in playing each other, and ending with their average point differential (the difference between their per-game averages for points scored and points yielded over the season). All playoff teams are awarded prize money, the amount increasing with each post-season game won.

Each year during a brief mid-season hiatus called the *all-star break*, the players selected as the best from the Eastern and Western conferences play each other in a special game called the *All-Star Game*. The All-Star Game players (known as *all-stars*) are selected by fan ballot as well as by each all-star coach (the coach of the most successful team in the conference over the first half of the season).

CHAPTER 6
College Basketball

College basketball in the United States is played according to rules that are virtually the same as those of the NBA, with only minor differences. The most important of these are highlighted below:

1. The college free-throw lane is twelve feet wide, as opposed to sixteen feet in the NBA (see illustration 1).
2. College basketball games consist of two twenty-minute halves, with no officially scheduled break until halftime—instead of four twelve-minute quarters, as in the NBA.
3. A college player is disqualified on his fifth personal foul—whereas in the NBA a player is permitted five personal fouls and is disqualified on his sixth.
4. A college team enters a penalty situation on its seventh team foul in a half—instead of on its fifth team foul in a quarter, as in the NBA.

5. As of this writing, some college conferences are experimenting with a three-point line similar to that used in the NBA; while in other college conferences there is no such line, and all field goals are worth two points. College three-point lines range from nineteen to twenty-two feet in distance from the basket.

6. In college basketball, defenders have no limit on how long they can remain in the lane, as they do in the NBA.

7. Zone defense, illegal in the NBA, is permitted in college basketball. There are several different zone defenses, whose names are usually descriptive of the particular player alignment used. For instance, a "two-one-two" zone puts a defender to each side of the basket, two defenders outside, and one defender in the middle; while a "three-two" zone puts a defender in front of the basket, a defender to each side of him, and two defenders outside. It is difficult to penetrate against a zone defense, because a would-be penetrator starting outside normally has to go through at least two different zones before he reaches the basket—and is thus likely to face at least two different defenders in the process. Consequently an offensive team facing a zone defense will normally try to get an open, outside shot or pass the ball to an open player cutting through the middle. The usual method of attacking a zone defense is to station several players around the *perimeter* (or *periphery*)— that is, around the outside perimeter of the front-court area being patrolled by defenders—while the remaining offensive players (usually the tallest) cut through the middle or set screens. The perimeter players pass the ball quickly back and forth to one another to confound the outermost defenders, who run back and forth in pursuit of the ball.

8. As of this writing, some college basketball conferences are experimenting with a shot clock similar to that used in the NBA, while others use no such clock and the offensive team can take as long as it likes to shoot. College shot clocks range in duration from thirty to forty-five seconds, and may be turned off in the last few minutes of the second half. A strategy sometimes used in the absence of a shot clock is the *slowdown* (or *freeze*, or *stall*, or *delay*), in which the offensive players dribble and pass the ball in the front court for a considerable length of time before shooting. Such a tactic is normally used only by a team that is ahead—the idea being to use up official playing time while preventing the opposing team from getting possession of the ball and scoring. It may also serve to force the opposing players from a zone defense into man-to-man coverage, against which it will be easier to penetrate for an easy shot. A man-to-man defense is more effective than a zone against a slowdown because in man-to-man, no player is left uncovered, whereas in a zone the opponents can keep away from the defenders merely by staying away from their zones, which generally don't extend beyond the limits of shooting range. A slowdown may also be used to keep the ball away from a much better team and thus prevent it from building an insurmountable scoring lead.

9. In those college basketball conferences that don't use a shot clock (and in some that do), a ball handler being guarded by a defender who is no more than six feet away is considered to be *closely guarded*, and there is a limit on how long he is permitted to retain possession of the ball. If this limit is exceeded, the ball is awarded to the opposing team. Such an infraction is called a *closely guarded situation*, and its governing rules make a distinction between two front-court areas: the *midcourt* and the *forecourt*. A player's midcourt is that part of his front court extending from the division line to an imaginary parallel line indicated by sideline hash marks twenty-eight feet from the baseline (see illustration 1); a player's forecourt is the rest of his front court. In general, a closely guarded situation is ruled if a closely guarded ball handler retains possession of the ball for five straight seconds in his own midcourt, or if he either holds or dribbles the ball (not in combination) for five straight seconds anywhere in his front court. There are two exceptions: a) if he dribbles from his midcourt into his forecourt, he is allowed to retain the ball for an additional four seconds from the time he enters the forecourt; and b) if he starts to dribble in his forecourt, he is allowed to retain possession of the ball for an additional four seconds from the time he ends his dribble. The NBA has no violation comparable to the closely guarded situation: an NBA ball handler has no limitation (other than the shot clock and 10-second rule) on how long he can hold or dribble the ball.

10. In college basketball, if an offensive player who is not in the act of shooting is fouled when the defensive team is in a penalty situation (or if such a foul puts the defensive team over the limit), the fouled player gets a *one-and-one* opportunity; that is, he shoots one free throw, plus a second free throw if he makes the first one. In the NBA, all non-technical fouls award two free throws, unless the foul occurs on a successful field goal.

11. If a college shooter commits a charging foul and makes his shot, the field goal is nullified only if the contact was made before the ball was released—whereas in the NBA, a charging foul by a shooter always nullifies any field goal that might be scored on the shot.

12. In college basketball, there are no jump balls after the opening jump. In situations that would require a jump ball under NBA rules, opposing college teams instead alternate in inbounding the ball. A painted *arrow* displayed at the scorer's table points in the offensive direction of the team whose turn it is to make the next such inbounds pass.

13. On a shot, college defenders are permitted to pin the ball against the backboard with their arm or hand, and to touch the ball after it has hit the backboard if it is neither on its downward flight, nor in the imaginary cylinder above the rim. In the NBA, it is always against the rules for a defender to pin a shot against the backboard, or to touch it after it has hit the backboard (while it still has a chance to carom into the basket).

14. There is no limitation on the total number of college players from either team who can stand in the lane spaces before a free throw; whereas NBA lane spaces can be occupied by no more than three defenders and two offensive players.

15. The college game clock doesn't stop automatically after every field goal scored in the last two minutes of an overtime period or the second half, as does the NBA game clock.

College basketball teams are classified into several divisions according to the general level of play, with the highest level being that of Division I, to which the major college teams belong. Within the divisions are various conferences. The college basketball season begins around the end of November and is followed by the respective division championship tournaments, which finish around the end of March. The most prestigious tournament is the NCAA (National Collegiate Athletic Association) Division I tournament, which selects as its participants those teams considered to be the best in the division—including the various conference champions.

CHAPTER 7
International Rules

Basketball played outside the United States follows a set of rules known as *international rules*, as does basketball played at the level of international competition. International rules, which differ slightly from NBA and U.S. college rules, are subject to revision every four years (corresponding to Olympic years). At the time of this writing, the major differences between U.S. and international rules are that under the latter:

1. The free-throw lane is about nineteen feet wide at the baseline, and tapers to about twelve feet wide at the foul line.
2. There is no defensive lane restriction.
3. Zone defense is permitted.
4. Games are played in two twenty-minute halves, with a ten-minute halftime intermission.
5. There is a 30-second shot clock.
6. Any player from either team may touch the ball

as soon as it has touched the basket on a shot—whether or not the ball is still touching the basket or is in the imaginary cylinder above the hoop—as long as the player himself does not touch the basket, and no part of the ball is actually within the basket.

7. All periods start with a jump ball.

8. If a player holds the ball for five straight seconds while his defender is within three feet of him, a jump ball is ruled.

9. On any foul that awards two free throws, the fouled team has the option of instead inbounding the ball.

10. If a player who is fouled while taking an unsuccessful shot misses either of his free throws, he is awarded one additional free throw.

11. No shots are ever awarded for an offensive foul, even if a penalty situation is in effect. An offensive foul always merely awards the ball to the other team.

12. A lane violation on the part of any offensive player except the free-throw shooter does not nullify a successful free throw.

13. A player is disqualified on his fifth foul—including technical fouls.

14. A technical foul awards two free throws if committed by a player who is in the game, and one free throw followed by possession of the ball if committed by a coach or substitute.

15. A team enters the penalty situation on its eighth foul (personal or technical) in a half. Overtime periods are considered part of the second half.

16. After a ball handler stops moving, he can only use his rearmost foot as a pivot foot.

17. If a player deliberately throws the ball against an opponent, causing the ball to go out of bounds, the opponent's team is awarded the ball.

18. An official normally doesn't handle the ball before an inbounds pass by a team in its own back court—which means that the ball is sometimes inbounded before the opposing players can assume their defensive positions.

19. A team is allowed only two timeouts per half and one per overtime period, and only a coach may request a timeout.

CHAPTER 8
Box Scores, Standings, and Statistics

BOX SCORES

Sample Box Score

Bullets 100, 76ers 97
PHILADELPHIA

	Min	FG	FT	R	A	PF	T
Erving	36	10-22	0-0	7	3	2	20
Iavaroni	20	4-8	0-1	6	2	1	8
Malone	43	8-15	9-13	14	1	3	25
Cheeks	25	3-8	2-2	0	4	3	8
Toney	20	2-6	4-4	2	2	2	8
Richardson	31	5-10	4-8	5	4	3	14
Edwards	21	2-7	1-2	1	2	0	5
Jones	28	4-10	1-1	6	0	4	9
Schoene	11	0-1	0-0	1	1	2	0
Cureton	5	0-0	0-0	4	0	1	0
Totals	**240**	**38-87**	**21-31**	**46**	**19**	**21**	**97**

WASHINGTON

	Min	FG	FT	R	A	PF	T
Ballard	38	4-12	7-8	9	7	1	15
Ruland	25	5-10	1-4	7	4	6	11
Mahorn	42	5-11	0-0	11	1	5	10
Collins	30	6-12	3-4	6	4	2	15
Johnson	17	5-7	3-4	0	3	2	13
Haywood	28	6-16	1-2	11	0	6	13
Warrick	31	4-12	0-0	4	3	3	8
Davis	10	3-6	0-0	4	0	1	6
Grevey	16	2-6	4-4	1	0	4	8
Batton	2	0-0	1-2	0	0	0	1
Terry	1	0-0	0-0	0	0	0	0
Totals	**240**	**40-92**	**20-28**	**53**	**22**	**30**	**100**

Philadelphia	27	17	27	26	97
Washington	27	24	24	25	100

Steals—Philadelphia 7 (Cheeks, Richardson 2), Washington 7 (Ruland, Mahorn 2). Turnovers—Philadelphia 15 (Malone 5), Washington 13 (Ruland, Mahorn 3). Technical fouls—Washington (illegal defense), Philadelphia Coach Cunningham, Philadelphia (illegal defense).

A—19,035 (sellout).

Basketball box scores are newspaper summaries of games, presented in a standardized format that may vary slightly from city to city. They are very easy to decipher. Directly below the final score are listed, by team, all the players who played in the game—with the home team listed below the visitors. For each team, the players are listed in the order of their appearance in the game, beginning with the starting players, who are usually listed in the following order: the two forwards first, followed by the center and then the two guards. The columns to the right of the players' names show various game statistics for each player, usually abbreviated as follows:

Min: Total minutes of official game time played.
FG: Field goals made and attempted, with the first number representing the former and the second, the latter. For example, "5-10" by a player's name

in this column means that he made five field goals out of ten attempts.

FT: Free throws made and attempted, with the first number representing the former and the second, the latter. For example, "7-8" by a player's name in this column indicates that he made seven free throws out of eight attempts.

R: Rebounds gathered.

A: Assists made.

PF: Personal fouls committed. A "6" by a player's name in this column indicates that he fouled out of the game.

T: Total points scored.

Below the players' names are listed the team totals for the above-mentioned categories. Below this are the teams' point totals for each quarter, followed by the game's final score—with the home team listed below the visiting team.

Below these lines may be a summary of the following statistical categories:

Three-point goals: Which players (if any) made three-point shots.

Steals: Team totals for steals made, with the player (or players) who made the most steals on each team listed in parentheses along with the number of steals he made.

Turnovers: Team totals for turnovers committed, with the player (or players) who committed the most turnovers on each team listed in parentheses along with his total turnovers.

Technical fouls: Which players, coaches, and/or teams (if any) committed technical fouls.

The final statistic presented in the box score is the total spectator attendance for the game, which is given after the letter "A".

A somewhat abbreviated box score, which may be

used in place of the kind just described, is very similar except that there are no columns, and after each player's name is listed his field goal statistics (made and attempted), free throw statistics (made and attempted), and total points scored.

UNDERSTANDING THE STANDINGS

The *standings* is a ranking of all of the teams in a division at any point in a season, based on each team's *won-lost record* (or *record*). A team's won-lost record is the total number of games it has won over a given period, along with the number of games it has lost. The number of wins is always given first, and is separated from the number of losses by a hyphen (when written) or by the word "and" (when spoken). For example, a record of "ten and six" (ten wins and six losses) is written as "10-6." A team's *won-lost percentage* is computed from its won-lost record by dividing the total victories by the total games played, and carrying the result to three decimal places. Thus, for example, a team with a 10-6 record would have a won-lost percentage of 10 divided by 16 = .625.

At any point during the season, or at its end, a team's place in the standings is determined by comparing its won-lost record with the won-lost records of the other teams in the division. The first-place team is the one with the greatest difference between total games won and total games lost (computed by subtracting the latter from the former). The other teams are ranked according to how many *games behind* first place they are.

One determines how many games behind first place a particular team is by following a four-step process: 1) Subtract the total number of games the team in question has won from the total number of games the first-place team has won (if the team in question has won more games than the first-place team—which is unlikely, but possible if the first-place team has played fewer games—the difference will be a negative number); 2) Subtract the total number of games the first-place team has lost from the total number of games the team in question has lost (this, too. could conceivably produce a negative number); 3) Add together the two figures obtained from steps 1 and 2 (if either is negative, remember that adding a negative number to a positive number actually involves subtraction); 4) Divide the result by two (thus, the smallest unit for measuring a team's place in the standings is the "half-game").

A team moves one full game closer to first place with every combination of its own win and the first-place team's loss, and falls one full game farther behind first place with every combination of its own loss and the first-place team's win. The team in first place at the end of the season is considered the division champion.

The abbreviations used in the standings are as follows:

W = total games won
L = total games lost
Pct. = won-lost percentage (generally, the higher the won-lost percentage, the higher a team's place in the standings)
GB = games behind first place (a dash in this column indicates that the team is in first place)

Sample Standings

	W	L	Pct.	GB
Team A	43	16	.729	—
Team B	37	24	.606	7
Team C	35	25	.583	8½
Team D	33	28	.541	11
Team E	23	38	.377	21
Team F	20	41	.328	24

STATISTICS

Following are some of the statistics kept in basketball for individual players:

Scoring: Average number of points scored per game.

Field-goal percentage: Obtained by dividing the total field goals attempted into the total field goals made. Thus, for example, a player who "goes five for ten" (i.e., who makes five field goals out of ten attempts) would have a field-goal percentage of 5 divided by 10 = .50, or 50 percent.

Free-throw percentage: Obtained by dividing the total free throws attempted into the total free throws made.

Rebounds: Average number of rebounds gathered per game.

Assists: Average number of assists made per game.

Blocked shots: Average number of opponents' shots blocked per game.

Steals: Average number of steals made per game.

CHAPTER 9
History

Unlike the other major team sports, which evolved gradually from much older games, basketball is of sudden and comparatively recent origins, having been deliberately invented in 1891 to fill a recreational vacuum. It is also the only major team sport that began in the United States.

Basketball came into being when Luther Gulick, head of the physical education department at the International YMCA Training School (now Springfield College) in Springfield, Massachusetts, asked a young instructor named James Naismith to devise a team game that could be played indoors during the winter months, when the weather was too cold for the various outdoor sports the students enjoyed. In response, Naismith—borrowing and modifying certain ideas from football, soccer, and other games—came up with what is essentially modern basketball.

Naismith originally asked for two boxes to be nailed

overhead at either end of the gymnasium as goals for his new game, but peach baskets were all that could be found. The object was to throw a soccer ball into one basket and prevent the opposing team from doing likewise with the other basket. It was against the rules to carry the ball, which could only be advanced by passing.

The new game was a huge and immediate success. The students loved it, and introduced it to other locales throughout the country when they returned home for Christmas vacation. Much to Naismith's surprise, within just a year of its invention, basketball was being played across the United States, from coast to coast, as well as in his native Canada.

The earliest baskets had bottoms, requiring the use of a ladder to remove the ball each time a shot was made. Soon wire baskets were introduced, and poles were used to push the balls out. Later, net bags were suspended from metal hoops, and were constructed in such a way that the ball could be dislodged by pulling an attached cord. Finally, around 1912, bottomless nets came into use.

At first there were no backboards, but the popular spectator practice of sitting in the balcony just behind the basket and leaning over to interfere with the ball during play prompted teams to adopt screens to prevent such conduct. It wasn't long before wooden backboards took the place of these screens, and glass boards became legal around 1908.

The ball itself went through a process of evolution. For the first few years, soccer balls were used, but in 1894 a larger ball, about thirty-two inches in circumference, was manufactured specifically for basketball. This size was later reduced to thirty inches.

While modern basketball remains at heart the same game Naismith invented in 1891, there have been a number of modifications and rule changes over the years. Some of the most important of these have been the standardization of five-man teams (1897); the development of dribbling as a means of advancing the ball (about 1900); the elimination of free throws as the penalty for every violation (1923); the establishment of the 10-second rule (1932); the elimination of a jump ball after each field goal and successful free throw (1937); and the introduction of the shot clock (1954).

Intercollegiate basketball began in the 1890s, for both men and women, and grew rapidly. The special rules that once set women's basketball apart from the men's game were abandoned by the early 1970s, and today at the college level men and women play by virtually identical rules.

Although the first professional basketball teams came into being in the 1890s, intercollegiate play reigned supreme until the emergence in 1946 of the Basketball Association of America (BAA), which in 1949 merged with another, older professional league, the National Basketball League (NBL), to form the National Basketball Association (NBA). In 1967 a rival professional league, the American Basketball Association (ABA), was formed, but disbanded after the 1975–76 season, with four ABA teams joining the NBA.

Within just two years of its invention, basketball was already being played in over a dozen countries. Men's basketball became an Olympic sport in 1936, and was joined by women's basketball in 1978. Today basketball is the most widespread sport in the world, being played in over 150 countries around the globe.

SOME ALL-TIME NBA GREATS OF THE PAST

Paul Arizin. Forward and guard, Philadelphia Warriors (1950–1962). A prolific scorer noted for his shooting accuracy, he ammassed a total of 16,266 points over his NBA career and played in ten All-Star Games.

Red Auerbach. Coach, Washington Capitals of the BAA and Tri-Cities Blackhawks of the NBA (1946–1950), Boston Celtics (1950–1966). Named the "greatest coach in the history of the NBA" by the Professional Basketball Writers' Association of America in 1980, he led the Boston Celtics to eight consecutive league championships and compiled a career NBA won-lost record of 938 wins and 479 losses.

A Spectator's Guide to Basketball

Rick Barry. Forward, Oakland Oaks, Washington Capitals, and New York Nets of the ABA; San Francisco Warriors, Golden State Warriors, and Houston Rockets (1968–1980). A great all-around player noted for his passing as well as his shooting, he averaged 24.8 points and 4.9 assists per game over his professional career.

Elgin Baylor. Forward, Minneapolis Lakers and Los Angeles Lakers (1958–1972). One of the greatest all-around forwards in basketball history, he once scored 71 points in a single game and averaged 27.4 points and 13.5 rebounds per game over his career.

Wilt Chamberlain. Center, Philadelphia Warriors, San Francisco Warriors, Philadelphia 76ers, and Los Angeles Lakers (1959–1973). Over seven feet tall, he was one of the most dominating players the sport has known, once scoring 100 points in a single game (during the 1961–62 season, in which he averaged 50.4 points per game). Over the course of his career, he averaged 30.1 points, 22.9 rebounds, and 4.4 assists per game.

Bob Cousy. Guard, Boston Celtics (1950–1963); Cincinnati Royals (1969–70 season). One of the game's most spectacular dribblers and passers, he averaged 18.4 points and 7.5 assists per game in his NBA career and played in thirteen All-Star Games.

John Havlicek. Forward and guard, Boston Celtics (1962–1978). A great all-around player known for his competitiveness and versatility, he averaged 20.8 points, 6.3 rebounds, and 4.8 assists per game over his career and played in thirteen All-Star Games.

Pete Maravich. Guard, Atlanta Hawks and New Orleans Jazz (1970–1979); Utah Jazz and Boston Celtics (1979–80 season). Known for his prolific scoring as well as for his skillful dribbling, he averaged 24.2 points per game over his career.

George Mikan. Center, Chicago American Gears and Minneapolis Lakers of the NBL, Minneapolis Lakers of the NBA (1946–1956). One of the all-time great centers, he totalled 11,764 points during his professional career and was voted "Player of the Half Century" by the *Associated Press*.

Bob Pettit. Forward and center, Milwaukee Hawks and St. Louis Hawks (1954–1965). A great scorer and rebounder, he averaged 26.4 points and 16.2 rebounds per game over his NBA career.

Oscar Robertson. Guard, Cincinnati Royals and Milwaukee Bucks (1960–1973). One of the greatest all-around players in the history of the sport, he was skilled at virtually every aspect of the game, including scoring, passing, rebounding, and defending. A twelve-time all-star, he averaged 25.7 points, 9.5 assists, and 7.5 rebounds per game over his NBA career.

Bill Russell. Center, Boston Celtics (1956–1969). A defensive wizard whose dominance and team-oriented play helped bring the Celtics eight straight NBA championships, he grabbed a total of 21,721 rebounds during his career, was voted to eleven all-star teams, and was named "Athlete of the Decade" in 1970 by the *Sporting News*.

Dolph Schayes. Forward and center, Syracuse Nationals (NBL, 1948–49 season; NBA, 1948–1963); Philadelphia Warriors (1963–64 season). A great rebounder and powerful scorer, he tallied 19,249 points and over 12,000 rebounds during the course of his professional career.

Jerry West. Guard, Los Angeles Lakers (1960–1973). One of the greatest all-around guards the sport has known, he had defensive skills to match his scoring prowess. Over the course of his career he averaged 27 points per game, once scoring 63 points in a single contest, and played in thirteen All-Star Games.

GLOSSARY

Italicized terms explained in previous chapters are not included here. Capitalized terms within definitions refer to other Glossary entries.

Air-Ball. An errant shot that misses both basket and backboard.

All-America (also "All-American"). A college player selected (by an annual poll of experts) as among the best college players for a given season. There are several different All-America polls each season.

Alley-Oop. An exciting play in which a LOB PASS is caught near the basket by a leaping player who then dunks the ball or lays it up before landing.

Back-Door Play. An offensive maneuver in which a player cuts to the basket behind the defenders' backs and receives a pass for a layup or dunk.

Bench. 1) A bench or row of individual seats situated ON THE SIDELINES, and on which sit a team's coaches and those players who aren't actively involved in the game. 2) A team's substitute (i.e., non-starting) players—who sit on the bench for at least part of the game, and are said to enter the game from *off the bench*. 3) To demote a starting player to substitute status for disciplinary reasons or because of dissatisfaction with his performance.

Benchwarmer. A substitute who seldom plays.

Blow a Team Out. To beat an opposing team by a very wide margin. A game in which a team is blown out is called a *blowout*.

Blowout. (see BLOW A TEAM OUT)

Boards. Short for "backboards"; used in reference to rebounding, as in "the team is getting beaten off the boards" (meaning the team is getting out-rebounded by its opponent).

Bomb. A shot taken at a considerable distance from the basket.

Bonus. (see BONUS SHOT)

Bonus Shot (also "Bonus"). In college basketball, the second free throw awarded to a player who makes the first free throw of a one-and-one opportunity.

Bonus Situation. The situation (with regard to free throws) of a team whose opponent is in a penalty situation.

Box-and-One. A defensive scheme in which four defenders play zone defense in a box-shaped alignment, and the other defender plays man-to-man. Such a defense is illegal in the NBA.

A Spectator's Guide to Basketball

Breakaway. An offensive sequence in which a player in his own back court breaks downcourt far ahead of the defenders, to shoot an uncontested layup or dunk.

Brick. A missed shot that is released with poor TOUCH and caroms off the basket or backboard with all the delicacy of a hurled brick.

Bucket. 1) The basket. 2) A field goal.

Cager. A basketball player.

Can a Shot. To make a shot.

CBA. (see Continental Basketball Association)

Cellar. Last place in the standings.

Center Jump. The opening jump, or a jump ball that begins an overtime period.

Charity Stripe (also "Stripe"). The free-throw line.

The Circle. The foul circle. The *top of the circle* is that part of the foul circle farthest from the basket, and is the same as the top of the KEY.

Coast to Coast. From one end of the court to the other; as in "he grabbed the rebound and drove coast to coast for a lay up."

College Draft. (see DRAFT)

College Rankings (also "Rankings"). The official ranking (by a poll of experts) of the top teams in a given college basketball division at any point in the season. There are several different ranking polls, each one updated regularly.

Common Foul. In college basketball, a personal foul that is not committed against a player who is in the act of shooting, and that is neither flagrant, intentional, nor part of a double or multiple foul.

Convert. 1) To make a free throw. 2) To score as the result of an assist—in effect, converting the pass into a field goal.

Continental Basketball Association (also "CBA" and "Continental League"). A minor professional basketball league in the United States.

Cords. The basket net.

Crash the Boards. To aggressively try for a rebound.

"D." Defense.

Dead Ball. A ball that is unplayable because of a temporary suspension of game action (as when, for example, an official calls a foul). A playable ball is said to be *live*.

Deny a Player the Ball. To guard an offensive opponent so closely that he can't get free to receive a pass from his teammates.

Discontinued Dribble. A double-dribble violation.

Dish Off. To pass the ball while driving to the basket.

Double-Overtime. A second overtime period, played when the first overtime period ends in a tie. A third overtime period is called *triple-overtime*.

Draft (also "College Draft"). The formal process whereby NBA teams choose (or *draft*) new players from the college ranks each year. The selection is conducted in turn—generally in reverse order of the teams' previous-season standings—and lasts for a fixed number of *rounds* (that is, complete cycles, during each of which every team gets a chance to pick an as-yet-unchosen player). However, a team can sell or trade its place in the choosing order for a given round. The more coveted the college player, the earlier (or "higher") he is chosen in the draft—with the most coveted players drafted in the *first round*.

English. Spin imparted to the basketball, which can affect the way in which it bounces off the floor or backboard.

Exhibition Game. A game whose outcome has no bearing on the official standings of the teams and the official records of the players. Each NBA team plays several pre-season exhibition games during the month of October.

Fadeaway (also "Fall-Away"). A shot in which the ball is released as the shooter moves away from the basket.

Fall-Away. (see FADEAWAY)

Feed a Player. To pass the ball to a teammate who has an opportunity to shoot.

Finger Roll. A very close-in shot in which the ball is released by rolling it off the fingertips with the palm turned upward.

First Round. (see DRAFT)

First String. The five starting players on a basketball team. A team's five most-used RESERVES constitute its *second string*, and its remaining reserves, the *third string*.

Flood a Zone. (see OVERLOAD A ZONE)

Follow-Up. A close-in shot taken by an offensive rebounder moving toward the basket.

Force a Shot. To determinedly take a shot despite being well guarded.

Four Corners. In the absence of a shot clock, a type of stalling offense in which a player is stationed at each of the four corners of the front court, with the fifth player somewhere in between.

Free Agent. A professional player who has no contractual obligation to play for a team, and is thus free to sign a playing contract.

Freelance. To react spontaneously and individualistically on offense, instead of running teamwork-oriented set plays.

Garbage. An easy close-in shot taken after the shooter has gotten an offensive rebound, or picked up a loose ball, near the basket.

Garbage Time. The closing moments of a game whose outcome has already been decided (because one team is winning by an insurmountable margin). Garbage time is so called because its play tends to be sloppy and individualistic.

General Manager. A high-ranking team official who makes trades, negotiates player contracts, and oversees day-to-day team operations.

Give-and-Go. An offensive maneuver in which a player passes the ball to a teammate and then immediately cuts for the basket to receive a quick return pass.

Glass. The glass backboard.

Goal. 1) A field goal. 2) The basket.

Gun (also "Gunner"). A player who tends to shoot the ball very frequently.

Gunner. (see GUN)

Halfcourt. 1) One-half of the basketball court, from division line to end line. 2) A slow-TEMPO style of play, characterized by a PATTERNED OFFENSE. 3) A variation on the game of basketball using a single basket, which serves both teams.

Handchecking. A defensive technique in which the defender keeps a hand on his opponent's body. If the hand impedes the opponent's progress, it is ruled a personal foul on the defender.

The Hardwood. The court floor.

Held Ball. A situation in which two opposing players share possession of the ball during game action. A held ball warrants a jump ball between the two players involved.

High Post. The tactical position of an offensive player (usually the center) who stands near the foul line.

Hit. (see HIT A SHOT)

Hit a Shot (also "Hit"). To make a shot.

The Hole. The basket.

Home-Court Advantage. The advantage of playing at home, where teams tend to win more games than they do on the road—probably in large part because of the psychological boost from the cheering of the home fans.

Home Stand. A series of consecutive games played at home.

Hoop. 1) The basket. 2) A field goal.

Hot Hand. A streak of shooting accuracy; as in "he has a hot hand," meaning he's been shooting very accurately.

Injured List. An official list of those injured players (if any) on a team whose names have been temporarily removed from the ROSTER while they recuperate.

"J." A jump shot.

Key. The keyhole-shaped area in front of each basket, consisting of the lane and foul circle. The *top of the key* is that part of the key farthest from the basket.

Lead Pass. A pass thrown downcourt ahead of a running teammate so that he can catch it without breaking stride.

Lineup. A list of the five players representing a team on the court during a game.

Live Ball. (see DEAD BALL)

Lob Pass (also "Lob"). A high, gently thrown, arcing pass.

Low Post. The tactical position of an offensive player (usually the center) who stands down low, just outside the lane.

Moving Pick. (see MOVING SCREEN)

Moving Screen (also "Moving Pick"). An offensive foul in which a player, while setting a screen, moves in any direction other than the direction and path of the opponent he is screening.

National Invitational Tournament. (see NIT)

NIT. The National Invitational Tournament, an annual post-season college tournament which invites as participants those Division-I teams considered the best from among the teams not participating in the NCAA tournament.

One-on-One. 1) A style of play in which the shooter attempts to score largely by his own efforts against

A Spectator's Guide to Basketball

his defender. 2) HALFCOURT basketball (i.e., using only one basket) played with one player to a team.

On the Sidelines. Situated beyond the sidelines, out of bounds.

Over and Back. A back-court violation.

Overload a Zone (also "Flood a Zone"). To move more offensive players into a particular area of a zone defense than there are available defenders.

Overplay. 1) To guard an opponent by standing slightly to one side of his path to the basket, in order to force him to head in the other direction. 2) To DENY A PLAYER THE BALL.

Palming. A violation in which a dribbler temporarily loses control of the ball as it bounces, and briefly carries it in the palm of his hand.

Passing Lanes. The imaginary pathways leading from a ball handler to those teammates he is most likely to pass to.

Patterned Offense (also "Pattern Offense" and "Set Offense"). A style of offensive attack characterized by a slow TEMPO and methodical set plays.

Pick and Roll. An offensive maneuver in which a player sets a pick and then immediately cuts to the basket to receive a pass.

Pick Off a Pass. To intercept a pass.

Pivot (also "Pivot Man"). A team's center.

Playbook. A notebook containing all of the plays in a team's repertoire.

Player-Control Foul. In college basketball, any offensive foul committed by a ball handler.

The Point. The point guard position.

Pop. To shoot.

Post (also "Post Position"). Either a HIGH or a LOW POST.

Post a Defender (also "Post Up a Defender"). To take an offensive position down low against a defender (usually a shorter one) and try to shoot over him for a field goal.

Post Up a Defender. (see POST A DEFENDER)

Pump Fake. A false shooting motion with the arms, made by a ball handler to deceive a defender.

Rankings. (see COLLEGE RANKINGS)

Regular Season. The official basketball season—as opposed to the post-season playoffs.

Regulation (also "Regulation Time"). The non-overtime portion of a basketball game.

Reject a Shot. To block a shot.

Reserve. A substitute (i.e., non-starting) player.

Road Trip. A series of consecutive games played on the road.

Rookie. A first-year professional basketball player.

Roster. A list of all the players on a team—including substitutes—who are eligible to play in games. League rules limit roster size.

Roundball. The game of basketball.

Scoreboard. A large, electronically operated, elevated board which displays the score, period, time remaining, and team fouls at basketball games. The letter "P" under team-foul totals indicates that the team in question is in a penalty situation—in which case a light usually goes on by the opposing team's name.

Scout. A team agent whose function is to obtain information about rival teams or to recruit new players.

Scrimmage. An informal practice game.

Second String. (see FIRST STRING)

Set Offense. (see PATTERNED OFFENSE)

Set Shot. A shot taken with both feet on the floor. Outside of free throws, the set shot is no longer used much in basketball, since it is more easily blocked than the jump shot.

Shooting Foul. 1) A defensive foul committed against a player who is in the act of shooting. 2) A foul that awards one or more free throws to the fouled player.

Sidelined. Temporarily unable to play because of an injury.

Sink a Shot. To make a shot.

Sixth Man. A substitute who plays approximately as many minutes per game as do his starting teammates, but whose role is to enter the game off the BENCH.

Snowbird. An easy, uncontested BREAKAWAY shot.

Spread the Defense. To create easily penetrable spaces between the defenders by stationing the offensive players far apart from one another in the front court.

Stick a Shot. To make a shot.

Stripe. (see CHARITY STRIPE)

Stuff. 1) To dunk the ball. 2) To block an opponent's shot.

Sub. A substitute (i.e., non-starting) player.

Swingman. A player who can play as either a forward or a guard.

Swish. A field goal in which the ball touches neither backboard nor hoop, and makes a "swishing" sound as it passes through the net.

Telegraph a Pass. To inadvertently reveal to the opposing defenders (by gaze or other body language) one's intention to pass the ball to a particular teammate—thus making the pass easy to intercept.

Tempo. The pace at which the offensive team brings the ball upcourt during a game. A fast tempo implies bringing the ball upcourt quickly, as in a fast-breaking style of play; while a slow tempo implies bringing the ball upcourt slowly and deliberately, as in a PATTERNED OFFENSE.

Third String. (see FIRST STRING)

Three-Point Play. An offensive sequence in which a shooter is fouled as he makes a field goal, and then makes the ensuing free throw as well, for a total of three points.

Throw the Ball Away. To inadvertently throw the ball out of bounds.

Touch. The delicacy of release which imparts accuracy to a shot. An accurate shooter is said to have a "good touch."

Touch Pass. A quickly executed pass in which the recipient of a preceding pass taps or bats the ball with his hands to a teammate without first catching the ball.

Training Camp. A professional team's pre-season period of practice and player tryouts. In the NBA, training camp takes place during the month of October.

Transition. A team's transition from offense to defense when the opposing team gains possession of the ball, or from defense to offense when the opposing team gives up possession. The quickest transition from defense to offense is the fast break.

Trap. A defensive maneuver in which two or more players aggressively guard a ball handler in an attempt to cause a turnover.

Triangle-and-Two. A defensive scheme in which three defenders play zone defense in a triangle-shaped alignment, and the other two play man-to-man. Such a defense is illegal in the NBA.

Triple-Double. A player's reaching double figures (i.e., ten or more) in each of three statistical categories—usually scoring, rebounding, and assists—for a single game. For example, scoring fifteen points, grabbing eleven rebounds, and making ten assists in a game constitutes a triple-double—which is a mark of an outstanding individual performance.

Triple-Overtime. (see DOUBLE-OVERTIME)

Twine. The basket net.

Two-Shot Foul. Any foul awarding two free throws.

Underneath. Underneath the basket.

Up Front. On a team's front line; as in "the team is strong up front," meaning it has a very good front line.

Up and Down. A violation in which a ball handler who has left his feet lands with the ball still in his possession.

Veteran. An experienced professional basketball player.

Waive a Player. (see WAIVER)

Waiver. A professional basketball team's relinquishment of its right to claim a player who has been *waived* (i.e., unconditionally released) by his own team. If no team in the league claims such a player, he becomes a FREE AGENT; if he is claimed, his new team is said to have obtained him *on waivers*.

Wing. A side portion of the court.

INDEX
see also Glossary

ABA	79
above	47
all-star break	61
all-star coaches	61
All-Star Game	61
all-stars	61
American Basketball Association	79
Arizin, Paul	79
arrow	66
assistant coaches	31
assists	38, 56
at home	17
Auerbach, Red	79
away	17
BAA	79
backboard	16, 20–21
back court (court area)	29
back court (guards)	34
back court (violation)	30
ball	15–16
ball handler	18
ball in play	27
banked shots	36
Barry, Rick	80
baselines	15
basket (hoop)	16, 20–21
Basketball Association of America	79
basket rim	20
baskets (field goals)	18
Baylor, Elgin	80
beating a defender	47
big forward	35
big guard	34
blocked shots	16, 21, 54
blocking	22
blocking out	49
boxing out	49

breaking	41
breaks	41
buzzer	17, 19, 20
calling an infraction	17–18
calls	17
carrying	18
center court	27
centers	33–35, 47–49
Chamberlain, Wilt	80
charging	22, 50–51
clearing out a side	40
clock	17, 30, 42
closely guarded situations	65–66
coaches	31–32
continuation	24
corners	35
cornermen	35
court	15
Cousy, Bob	80
covering an opponent	45–46
cutting	37
defenders	16–17
defense	16
defensive fouls	22
defensive rebounding	42
delays	65
disqualifications	22
division line	29
double-clutching	40
double-dribble	18
double fouls	23, 28
double-pumping	40
doubleteaming	47
downcourt	34
dribbling	16, 18, 55–56
driving	34, 56
dunks	19, 36, 53–54
ejections	25
end lines	15
faking/faking out	40
falling off a man	47
fast breaks	41–42, 54–55
the field	25
field goals	18–19
filling a lane	42
five-second violations	20
the floor	25
forecourt	65
forwards	33–35
foul circles	27
fouling out	22
foul lanes	25–26
foul lines	25

fouls	22–25
foul shots	23, 25–26
free-throw circles	27, 28
free-throw lanes	25–26
free-throw lines	25
free throws	23, 25–26
free-throw violations	26
freezes	65
from the field	25
from the floor	25
front court	29
fronting a player	46
front line	35
full-court presses	50
game clock	17, 30
games behind	74
goaltending	21
guarding an opponent	38, 45–46
guards	33–35
Gulick, Luther	77
half-court	29
half-court presses	50
halftime	17
halves of a game	17
handling the ball	18
hash marks	32, 51
Havlicek, John	80
head coaches	31
helping out	47–48
high	35
home team	17
hooks	36
hook shots	36
hoop	16
horn	17
illegal defense	51
inbounding	19–20
in bounds	15
inbounds passes	19–20
in play	27
inside	35
inside lane	48
interference	21
jams	19
jump balls	27–28, 32
jump circle	27
jumpers	36
jump shots	36
lanes	25–26
lane-space marks	26
lane spaces	26
lane violations	26

laying the ball up	36
lay-ins	36
layups	36
the limit	23
the line	25
loose ball fouls	22, 24
low	35
man (a players')	46
man-for-man	46
man-to-man defense	46
Maravich, Pete	80
match-ups	38
midcourt (court area; college basketball)	65
midcourt (line)	29
middle	47
Mikan, George	81
mini-series	60
mismatches	38
moves	40
Naismith, James	77–78
National Basketball League	79
National Collegiate Athletic Association	67
NBL	79
NCAA	67
net	20
offense	16
offensive fouls	22
offensive interference	21
offensive rebounding	42
off guard	34
officials	17, 20, 32
official scorer	24, 31
officials' signals	32
off the ball	24, 28
one-and-one	66
one-on-one play	39–40
on the ball	28
on the road	17
open	34
opening jump/tap/tip/tip-off	27
options	39
outlet passes	41
out of bounds	15, 19, 20, 21
outrebounded	43
outside	34
outside lane	48
over the limit	23
overtime	17, 28
paint	26
paint area	26
passes	16, 18
penalty situations	23
penetrating	34

perimeter	64
periods	17
periphery	64
personal fouls	22–25
personals	22
Pettit, Bob	81
picked off	37
picks	37
pivot foot	18
player positions	33–35
playing time	43
paymaker	34–35
playmaking guard	34–35
playoffs	60
play (game action)	17
plays	39
point guard	34
points	16
possession	19
position	49
positions of players	33–35
power forward	35
presses	50
quarters	17
rebounding	21, 42, 49–50, 56
rebounds	21
record	74
referees	17, 20, 32
regular timeouts	31
regulation-length game	31
restraining circle	27, 28
rim	20
road	17
Robertson, Oscar	81
running a play	39
running out the clock	42
Russell, Bill	81
Schayes, Dolph	81
scorer's table	24, 31
screens	37
set plays	39
shooting	16, 36–37, 55
shooting guard	34–35
shooting over an opponent	38
shot clock	29
shots	16
sidelines	15
slam-dunks	19
slams	19
slowdowns	64–65
small forward	35
stalls	65
standings	74
starters	43

starting players	43
steals	16–17
steps	18
strong forward	35
strong side	47
stuffs	19
substitutions of players	31, 43
switching	46
tap-ins	19
taps	19
team fouls	23–24
teamwork	40, 57–58
technical fouls	24–25, 51
technicals	24
10-second line	29
10-second violations	30
three-point lines	19
three-point shots	19, 32
3-second lanes	26
three seconds (violation)	26
throw-ins	19–20
time	31
timeline	29
timeouts	30–31
timers	24
timing the game	17, 30
tip-ins	19, 42
tip-off circle	27
tip-off	27
tips	19
trailer	42
traveling	18
"T"s	24
turning the ball over	43
turnovers	43
24-second clock	29
24-second rule	29
20-second timeouts	31
uniforms of players	32
upcourt	34
using up the clock	42
violations	30
visiting team	17
visitors	17
walking	18
weak side	47
West, Jerry	81
whistles (officials')	17
won-lost percentage	74
won-lost record	74
zone	46
zone defense	46, 48, 51, 64, 65